Miracles Beyond Our Comprehension

Miracles Beyond Our Comprehension

A. M. Deigloriam

RESOURCE *Publications* • Eugene, Oregon

Resource Publications
An Imprint of Wipf and Stock Publishers
199 W. 8th Ave., Suite 3
Eugene, OR 97401

www.wipfandstock.com

PAPERBACK ISBN: 978-1-4982-9674-8
HARDCOVER ISBN: 978-1-4982-9676-2
EBOOK ISBN: 978-1-4982-9675-5

Manufactured in the U.S.A.   JULY 15, 2016

Dedicated to my loving wife of forty-four years, my family, and my many friends

Table of Contents

Introduction

We live at a time when many of the values this country was founded on are no longer followed and our society and its related legal decisions are a drift and being based on current social values and political correctness. Throughout history great countries and their societies have come and gone due to internal corruption and moral decay. Our society and the government are no longer willing to recognize the value of the church and how God has blessed this country over many years. The national and local media no longer uses words that reference God's blessings or how Satan's influences are destroying society and the family. Society and the government do not recognize or understand the relationship between Satan, disease, death and sin. Nor do they understand the relationship between obedience to God's word and God's protection.

We see a great deal of unrest today, as different religious groups throughout the world view the United States as the great demon that is continually distributing offensive television programs, movies and other perverse materials. Throughout history different religious beliefs have been involved in creating strife between people and in some cases starting wars. Many of the wars and conflicts in the past was the result of unjust treatment of certain countries or groups of people. Unfortunately, we can also point to certain individuals of the past that were responsible for barbaric acts of genocide. There is no possible explanation for these barbaric acts other than to acknowledge Satan is able to control man by offering him great power and wealth. This is the same Satan that transported Jesus to the top of a mountain and offered Him control over all the earth. Radical Islamic terrorists are also following a belief that all people should be conforming to their beliefs and that they will receive great blessings for their efforts regardless of the cost to innocent people.

As the world continues to deteriorate in moral decay, man's actions will follow Satan's path to self destruction.

Satan and his demons are extremely powerful, cunning, and cruel principalities that we need to be aware of each day. We cannot let our guard down or underestimate his influences with regards to our attitudes, values, priorities, and love for our neighbor. We see children killing children in our cities and there is little or no response on the part of the church or the government. The country is so numb to news of more acts of violence they no longer feel sorrow or compassion for those families that have been destroyed. Satan and his demons have confused man to the point to where he rationalizes all these acts of pure evil as acts caused by a logical response, or by those with a mental illness.

The world today does not believe in the existence of God or Satan and refuses to believe Satan is actively involved in death, disease and sin. The Christian through the death and resurrection of Christ has experienced God's grace and know God provides protection against Satan and his demons on a daily basis through the obedience to his word.

The miracles completed by Jesus and his disciples were miracles that gave sight to the blind, healed those with leprosy, feed the hungry, raised some from the dead, healed many other infirmities and healed those possessed by demons.

Jesus during his three year ministry confronted Satan and many of his demons. In one case it is believed that one man was possessed by over 6,000 demons. The result of this possession was a man that was driven to insanity. We need to remember Satan and demons are still active today in the dark shadows and we see their work on a daily basis throughout the world.

However, we also need to remember that all of God's promises were fulfilled in Christ and that we were sealed by the Holy Spirit.

The Holy Spirit sealed us and took ownership of our souls. The Holy Spirit provides security, ownership, and a pledge of redemption.

2 Corinthians 1:20-24 reads, For all the promise of God in him are yea, and in him Amen, unto the glory of God by us. Now he which stablisheth us with you in Christ, and hath anointed us in God; Who hath also sealed us, and given the earnest of the Spirit in our hearts. Moreover I call God for a record upon my soul, that to spare you I came not as yet unto Corinth. Not for that we have dominion over your faith, but are helpers of your joy: for by faith ye stand.

We are a vessel that receives Christ and all the promises made by God for us.

The Fall

ADAM'S DISOBEDIENCE RESULTED NOT only in a physical death but also in the separation from God for all of mankind. This disobedience brought all of mankind to its knees in death and suffering. The only possible release from this curse of death and suffering was the death and suffering of God's Son. It is this Grace given freely by God that we are able gain our salvation within this fallen world. With faith, obedience, and God's Grace we live each day in anticipation of His return.

Man is responsible for yielding to sin and Satan and to the demon power that brings all kinds of failures and sufferings. Man lives a life that is lustful and unclean, which breeds sickness and disease. Sins of all kinds, fleshly lusts, pride, unbelief, and many other acts of man may cause a break in God's laws. This break in God's law may provide Satan the opportunity to inflict great pain in an individual's life. Satan may take advantage when he feels the time is right. Those who sow will have to reap.

And unto Adam he said, Because thou hast hearkened unto the voice of thy wife, and hast eaten of the tree, of which I commanded thee, saying, Thou shalt not eat of it; cursed is the ground for thy sake; in sorrow shalt thou eat of it all the days of thy life. Thorns also and thistles shall it bring forth to thee; and thou shalt eat the herb of the field. In the sweat of thy face shalt thou eat bread, till thou return unto the ground; for out of it wast thou taken: for dust thou art, and unto dust shalt thou return. Genesis 2: 17-19.

The fall of mankind also resulted in Satan becoming a powerful force in executing sin, sickness, and death in the daily life of each individual. The following verses provide additional explanations of Satan's influences and the demons each individual encounters each day.

I John 3:8 reads, He that committeth sin is of the devil; for the devil sinneth from the beginning. For this purpose the Son of God was manifested, that he might destroy the works of the devil.

Matthew 12:22- 28 reads, Then was brought unto him one possessed with a devil, blind, and dumb: and he healed him, insomuch that the blind and dumb both spake and saw. And all the people were amazed, and said, Is not this the son of David? But when the Pharisees heard it, they said, This fellow doth not cast out devils, but be Beelzebub the prince of the devils. And Jesus knew their thoughts, and said unto them, "Every kingdom divided against itself is brought to desolation; and every city or house divided against itself shall not stand. And if Satan cast out Satan, he divided against himself; how shall then his kingdom stand? And if by Beelzebub cast out devils, by whom do your children cast them out? Therefore they shall be your judges. But if I cast out devils by the Spirit of God, then the kingdom of God is come unto you."

The possession of this demon caused the blindness and dumbness of this man. Even the Pharisees recognized that Satan was responsible for this illness and were accusing Jesus of working with Beelzebub to cast out demons and heal this man. Jesus and his kingdom have no room for Satan and his demons.

John 10:10 reads, "The thief cometh not, but for to steal, and to kill, and to destroy: I am come that they might have life, and that they might have it more abundantly."

Jesus is the good shepherd that watches over his flock to protect them from the evil one and his workers. Satan's primary focus is to destroy, to steal, and to use disease and death for his purpose.

Ephesians 2:1-3 reads, And you hath he quickened, who were dead in trespasses and sins; Wherein time past ye walked according to the course of this world, according to the prince of the power of the air, the spirit that now worketh in the children of disobedience. Among whom also we all had our conversation in times past in the lust of our flesh, fulfilling the desires of the flesh and the mind; and were by nature the children of wrath, even as others.

Paul is praying in these verses that the church and all of mankind realize that God has given them life and more then they can comprehend. Before the conversion of the Church of Ephesians these people were following the philosophies, values, and life styles of all those who followed Satan. There were no spiritual laws that provided direction and consequently they lived with no concept of evil and good.

Hebrews 2: 14-15 reads, Forasmuch then as the children are partakers of flesh and blood, he also himself likewise took part of the same; that through death he might destroy him that had power of death, that is, the devil. And deliver them who through fear of death were all their lifetime subject to bondage.

Jesus took on the body of a man and settled the issue of sin with His death and resurrection. He became flesh and blood and therefore died, but with His death came deliverance from sin. Therefore the fear of death is gone for the believer, since they have been set free of Satan and bondage of a spiritual death.

Acts 10:38 reads, How God anointed Jesus of Nazareth with the Holy Spirit and with the power: who went about doing good, and healing all that were oppressed of the devil; for God was with Him.

Peter's preaching presents a clear message of the Bible and how he lived a sacrificial life. Jesus was the anointed messenger that worked in the healing and the exorcism of demons.

We need to ask the question how can we be trusted if we can't manage a life that consists of a wealth of blessings. We have been given these small fragile bodies that may be extinguished at any time. How are we using this time and these bodies to glorify God?

Jesus revealed his compassion for man as he shed tears at the grave of Lazarus and sweated blood in Gethsemane. It was God's ultimate sacrifice that broke Satan's hold and provided a way for salvation. We are baptized into the death of Jesus and given the gift of salvation.

Jesus and His mission

JOHN 3:16-18 READS, FOR God so loved the world, that he gave his only begotten Son, that whosoever believeth in him should not perish, but have everlasting life. For God sent not his Son into the world to condemn the world; but that the world through him might be saved. He that believeth on him is not condemned; but he that believeth not is condemned already, because he hath not believed on the name of the only begotten Son of God.

God's first priority was to send us his son to pay for our sins and to release us from the law. However, to receive this salvation man needs to believe that God did make this sacrifice for us so that we may have eternal life.

Romans 8: 3-4 reads, For what the law could not do, in that it was weak through the flesh, God sending his own Son, in the likeness of sinful flesh, and for sin, condemned sin in the flesh. That righteousness of the law might be fulfilled in us, who walk not after the flesh, but after the Spirit.

We need to remember that all healings of these bodies are completed by God, not merely that his providence provided medical assistance, but that the fact that our very tissues are healed by God's energy flowing from the first moment of life and his creation.

We were created in his likeness and a faint image of the Divine Incarnation. God indwells into our spirit and our senses, thoughts and emotions. We will also grow in appreciation of all he has done for us not only in all the daily blessings, but in our families, friends, and all the natural state of being that exists on this earth.

The incarnation of God becoming man is beyond our comprehension. It is this miracle that all other miracles point to and allow us some sight into his glory. He allowed his eternal spirit to be combined with a human that he created from dust and breathed into him the breath of life.

Genesis 2:7 reads, And the Lord God formed man of the dust of the ground, and breathed into his nostrils the breath of life; and man became a living soul.

At this time man received the life breath of God and became a soul. Man is therefore a creature of two worlds both earth and heaven. Two miracles occurred at this time, the formation of a body from dust and the life that was created by the divine breath of God. This being was given free will and the ability to reason, feel, discern, and to communicate and develop their own character.

These miracles were acts of love within the reality that exist here on earth and in God's eternal universe. God is by definition love and has a plan and will provide for those of faith on this small planet. This love was revealed in the death of His son and will exist as love for all of eternity. God existed before the human race and will exist even after the earth becomes nothing.

The Birth of Jesus into Poverty

JESUS THE SON OF God was born not as a king with pomp and circumstances but in poverty and as an outcast of men. He was born in a manger for cattle and was wrapped in swaddling clothes (rags). Jesus would live in poverty for his entire life and would never be rich in material goods. God provided Jesus with his daily needs for shelter, food and clothing. Jesus told his disciples in Luke 9:58, Foxes have holes, and birds of the air have nests; but the Son of man hath not where to lay his head. We need to remember that Gods' riches are not material riches.

Jesus was born in the small village of Bethlehem and not in Jerusalem. The wise men first traveled to Jerusalem thinking a king that would restore the kingdom of David would certainly be born in Jerusalem where the temple was located. He came into the world in love and in willing obedience to God. He was born of flesh, like any other man so that he may bore the sin of the flesh and died on the cross.

Jesus was born as an outcast and would remain an outcast his entire life. His life was in danger soon after his birth in the small village of Bethlehem. King Herod after hearing of the prophecy of a new king and the birth sent out soldiers to kill the baby Jesus. Even today people reject Jesus and consider him to be a threat and an outcast.

Jesus was born of Mary a virgin and was God in flesh. Due to the fact that Jesus was the first born he was to be consecrated to God and was to be devoted to the service of God in the temple.

However, Jesus was the first born of God and Mary and would be devoted to being the Savior of the world.

God could have allowed Jesus to be born in a mansion with great wealth and many servants befitting a king. Why would God allow his only begotten son not only be born in a shed for cattle but in poverty as well and in danger of being slain by Herod?

The birth of Jesus and the status of his birth are directly related to the requirements needed to fulfill God promises to mankind. God's example to us is the life of Jesus. A man who's only purpose in life was to fulfill God's plan that would provide eternal life for his chosen people that believe him and obey his commandments.

Luke 16:19-24 reads, "There was a certain rich man, which was clothed in purple and fine linen, and fared sumptuously every day. And there was a certain beggar named Lazarus, which was laid at his gate, full of scores. And desiring to be fed with the crumbs which fell from the rich man's table: moreover the dogs came and licked his sores. And it came to pass, that the beggar died, and was carried by the angel into Abraham's bosom: the rich man also died, and was buried. And in hell he lifted up his eyes, being in torments, and seeth Abraham afar off, and Lazarus in his bosom. And he cried and said, Father Abraham, have mercy on me, and send Lazarus that he may dip the tip of his finger in water, and cool my tongue; for I am tormented in this fame."

We need to show respect to all men regardless of their wealth or standing in society. We honor them because their souls are of more value than all the wealth in the world. This rich man walked by this beggar at his gate each day and only offered crumbs off his table. This beggar was created in God's image and was dependent on others for love. John 13: 34-35 reads, A new commandment I give unto you. That ye love one another; as I have loved you, that ye also love one another. By this shall all men know that ye are my disciples, if ye have love one to another.

Isaiah 8:13 reads, Sanctify the Lord of hosts himself; and let him be your fear, and let him be your dread.

We fear an all-powerful God that allows us to take each breath and requires us to love one another and obey his commandments.

1 Timothy 6:17-19 reads, Charge them that are rich in this world, that they be not highminded, nor trust in uncertain riches, but in the living God, who giveth us richly all things to enjoy. That they do good, that they be rich in good works, ready to distribute, willing to communicate. Laying up in store for themselves a good foundation against the time to come, that they may lay hold on eternal life.

With wealth comes great responsibility. Those that have been blessed with wealth must share that wealth generously with the poor. There is a callous attitude among some that wealth is a sign of God's favor and that the poor have done something to deserve their condition. 1 John 3:17 reads, But whose hath this worlds good, and seeth his brother have need, and shutteth up his bowels of compassion from him, how dwelleth the love of God in him?

Wealth is not given for the purpose building mansions, purchasing expensive cars or expensive works of art, but for the purpose of serving the poor and providing for those that are in need. God will severely judge those with wealth that do not provide for the poor and do not show his love for their neighbors.

Jesus did not declare wealth a sign of God's favor or that poverty is God's punishment for doing something wrong. Jesus saw wealth as a gift that should be used to help the poor and to show God's love.

The Childhood of Jesus

THE GOSPELS TELL US little about Jesus during his childhood. After the birth of Jesus, King Herod, hearing that a king was born sent out a decree to kill young babies. The young family was forced to flee for their lives and escaped to Egypt where they stayed until the death of Herod.

Matthew 2:13-16 reads, And when they were departed, behold the angel of the Lord appeareth to Joseph in a dream, saying, Arise, and take the young child and his mother, and flee into Egypt, and be thou there until I bring thee word for Herod will seek the young child to destroy him. When he arose, he took the young child and his mother by night, and departed into Egypt. And was there until the death of Herod: that it might be fulfilled which was spoken of the Lord by the prophet, saying, Out of Egypt have I called my son. Then Herod, when he saw that he was mocked of the wise men, was exceeding wroth, and sent forth, and slew all the children that were in Bethlehem, and all the coasts thereof, from two years old and under, according to the time which he had diligently inquired of the wise men.

The death of Herod occurred about 4 B.C. Herod was a man of great barbarity and his son Archelaus was as brutal as his father.

Matthew2: 19-23 reads, But when Herod was dead, behold, an angel of the Lord appeareth in a dream to Joseph in Egypt. Saying, Arise, and take the young child and his mother, and go into the land of Israel: for they are dead which sought the young child's life. And he arose, and took the young child and his mother, and came into the land of Israel. But when he heard that Archelaus did reign in Judea in the room of his father Herod, he was afraid to go thither: notwithstanding, being warned of God in a dream, he turned aside into the parts of Galilee. And he came and dwelt in the city called Nazareth: that it might be fulfilled which was spoken by the prophets, He shall be called a Nazarene.

Joseph was directed by God to move to Egypt for a few years and live there with Mary and Jesus until it was safe to return to Israel. Once Herod was dead God again appeared to Joseph and directed him to return to Israel and to avoid the son of Herod, Archelaus. They eventually ended up in Nazareth where Jesus spent his childhood.

Luke 2: 40-51 reads, And the child grew, and waxed strong in spirit, filled with wisdom, and the grace of God was upon him. Now his parents went to Jerusalem every year at the feast of the Passover. And when he was twelve years old, they went up to Jerusalem after the custom of the feast. And when they fulfilled the days, as they returned, the child Jesus tarried behind in Jerusalem: and Joseph and his mother knew not of it. But they, supposing him to have been in the company went a day's journey; and they sought him among their kinsfolk and acquaintance. And when they found him not, they returned back again to Jerusalem, seeking him. And it came to pass, that after three days they found him in the temple, sitting in the midst of the doctors, both hearing them, and asking them questions. And all that heard him were astonished at his understanding and answers. And when they saw him, they were amazed: and his mother said unto him, Son, why hast thou thus dealt with us? Behold thy father and I sought thee sorrowing. And he said unto them, "How is it that ye sought me? Wist ye not that I must be about my Father's business?". And they understood not the saying which he spake unto them. And he went down with them, and came to Nazareth, and was subject unto them: but his mother kept all these sayings in her heart. And Jesus increased in wisdom and stature, and in favor with God and man.

We know from this account Jesus at the age of twelve was already confronting the wise men (rabbis, teachers) of the day with questions and answers. Joseph and Mary must have been completely exhausted from looking for Jesus for three days. And, we see that Jesus was in submission to them as they returned to Nazareth. We also need to remember Jesus took on the nature of God and the nature of his parents and continued to grow both physically and spiritually in Nazareth and along the Sea of Galilee.

Jesus grew up in a family with both brothers and sisters. The brothers are named in a number of places within the Bible.

Matthew 13:55 reads, Is not this the carpenter son? Is not the mother called Mary? and his brethren, James, and Joses, and Simon, and Judas (Jude). And his sisters, are they not all with us? Whence then hath this man all these things?

There is not a lot of information about the family. However, it is commonly believed that both James and Judas were writers of the New Testament epistles. It also believed that one of Jesus' sister married and stayed in Nazareth before the family moved to Capernaum.

It is believed that Joseph died before Jesus started his ministry and before the Crucifixion. The last time Joseph is mentioned is at the temple in Jerusalem where Jesus was found with the rabbis and wise men of the day.

Jesus as an Adult

THE MINISTRY OF JESUS starts with his baptism by John the Baptist when he was about 30 years old.

Mark 1:11 reads, And it came to pass in those days, that Jesus came from Nazareth of Galilee, and was baptized of John in Jordan. And straightway coming up out of the water, he saw the heavens opened, and the Spirit like a dove descending upon him. And there came a voice from heaven, saying, thou art my beloved Son, in whom I am well pleased.

John the Baptist's primary purpose in life was to fulfill the prophecy which is to prepare the way for Jesus. John was chosen to baptize Jesus and to fulfill the prophecy.

The second time the voice of God was heard was at the transfiguration of Jesus on the mountain with three disciples (Peter, John, and James) as witnesses. Those that were present on top of the mountain were Moses, Elijah, Jesus, Peter, John and James.

Mark 9:2 reads, And after six days Jesus taketh with him Peter, and James, and John, and leadeth them up into a high mountain apart by themselves: and he was transfigured before them. And his raiment became shining, exceeding white as snow; so as no fuller on earth can white them. And there appeared unto them Elijah with Moses: and they were talking with Jesus. And Peter answered and said to Jesus, Master, it is good for us to be here: and let us make three tabernacles; one for thee, and one for Moses, and one for Elijah. For he wist not what to say; for they were sore afraid. And there was a cloud that overshadowed them: and a voice came out of the cloud saying, This is my beloved Son: hear him.

At this point, God transformed Jesus by matching the outside and inside of the body of Jesus. The glory of God was revealed in Jesus.

Hebrew 10:20 reads, By a new and living way, which he hath consecrated for us, through the veil, that is to say, his flesh.

Jesus Christ is the new and living way in which believers have direct access into the very Holy place of God.

Philippians 2: 7 reads, But made himself of no reputation, and took upon him the form of a servant, and was made in the likeness of man.

Jesus recognized sinners to be more important than Himself and was concerned with their needs. Jesus came to this earth in the form of a man to be the true servant of God and to provide the greatest gift, eternal life.

Miracles

JESUS BLESSED HIS PEOPLE with many miracles for many reasons. He revealed His compassion and mercy with many miracles that were related to the healing of infirmities that people were suffering with for many years. Chief among these reasons for these miracles was the training of the twelve disciples. The disciples had to learn that faith in God was the source for power in accomplishing great tasks.

Jesus conducted hundreds if not thousands of miracles during a three year period, but only a few were recorded as outlined below. Many people received the mercy of Jesus as he healed them of their many health issues, demon possession, and other spiritual issues. However, there were five distinct instances where Jesus offended Jewish law by healing people on the Sabbath. Those miracles were of mercy and included healing a man of palsy, a withered hand, blindness, dropsy, and a woman with an infirmity for over 18 years. One could make the point the Pharisees were acting faithfully in accordance with their theoretical views by finding fault with Jesus, but they made no allowance for mercy for those in need on the Sabbath.

The more we understand who God is and comprehend His love, power, presence, the more credible the miracles become. These miracles express God's beauty, truth, and goodness that lives within our beings that needs to be expressed through us on a daily basis.

The Approximate Beginning of Jesus' First Year of Ministry

JESUS WAS ABOUT THIRTY year old when he travels from his home town of Nazareth to Galilee. He begins His ministry with being baptized by John the Baptist. During this first year He is confronted by Satan and is tested and begins His ministry with miracles. He begins to spend time selecting His disciples and training them. He then left Galilee to be baptized at the Jordan River. It was here that he met John the Baptist that was prophesized 400 years prior in the Book of Malachi.

Malachi 4:5-6 reads, Behold, I will send you Elijah the prophet before the coming of the great and dreadful day of the Lord. And he shall turn the heart of the fathers to the children, and the heart of the children to their fathers, least I come and smite the earth with a curse.

We are to keep the law of Moses and the message that John the Baptist presented throughout his life that prepared for the coming of Christ the Savior. Through John the Baptist and God men were brought to the repentance of their sins, conversion, and obedience to God's word.

John 1:29 reads, The next day John seeth Jesus coming unto him, and saith, Behold the lamb of God, which taketh away the sin of the world. John saw the Holy Spirit descend on Jesus and realized that Jesus was the Lamb of God, the Son of God, the one that would be sacrificed for all the sins of mankind.

John the Baptist is believed to have disciples that were transferred to Jesus' ministry (One is identified as Andrew). Other early disciples that appear at this time are James, Phillip, Peter, and, Bartholomew.

Immediately after Jesus' baptism, he is directed by God's spirit into the wilderness for forty days to be confronted by Satan and to be ministered by angels. Jesus is obedient to God's will and comes face to face with Satan and is attacked in a way that no ordinary man could endure. However, Jesus was a divine being that could not sin.

Matthew 4:3-11 reads, And when the tempter came to him, he said, If thou be the Son of God, command that these stones be made bread. But he answered and said, "It is written. Man shall not live by bread alone, but by every word that proceedeth out of the mouth of God." Then the devil taketh him up into the holy city, and setteth him on a pinnacle of the temple. And saith unto him, If thou be the Son of God, cast thyself down: for it is written, He shall give his angels charge concerning thee: and in their hands they shall bear thee up, lest at any time thou dash thy foot against a stone. Jesus said unto him, "It is written again, Thou shalt not tempt the Lord thy God." Again, the devil taketh him up into an exceeding high mountain, and showeth him all the kingdoms of the world, and the glory of them. And saith unto him, All these things will I give thee, if thou wilt fall down and worship me. Then saith Jesus unto him, "Get thee hence, Satan: for it is written, Thou shalt worship the Lord thy God, and Him only shalt thou serve." Then the devil leaveth him, and, behold, angels came and ministered unto him.

Jesus experienced his life as a deity/human from birth to death and allowed himself to be experience the tests of Satan for forty days while fasting in the wilderness.

Hebrews 1:13-14 reads, But to which of the angels said he at any time, Sit On My Right Hand, Until I Make Thine Enemies Thy Footstool? Are they not all ministering spirits, sent forth to minister for them who shall be heirs of salvation?

The angels have always been principally involved in carrying out many ministries for both God and his Son. These ministries have included giving the Mosaic law, delivering messages from God, performing miracles, protecting children and for providing many more blessings. Jesus was made a little lower than the angels so that he may taste death for every man. It was his suffering as a deity and human that justified him and resulted in him being exalted and crowned with glory.

Satan attacks Jesus realizing the outcome, but he still attacks. Satan also realizes Jesus has fasted for forty days and his human body must be weak from the lack of food. Jesus' reply is from Deuteronomy 8:3, Man shall not live by bread alone, but be every word that proceedeth out of the mouth of God. Jesus' source of strength was his obedience to the Father's will. The importance of obedience and being in God's will cannot be minimized.

Satan uses Psalm 91:11 reads, For he shall give his angels charge over thee, to keep thee in all thy ways. Satan is asking Jesus to sin by testing God. Jesus reply is from Deuteronomy 6:16, Ye shall not tempt the Lord your God, as ye tempted him in Massah.

Satan's third temptation is to offer many kingdoms to Jesus if he would worship him. At this point, Jesus rebukes Satan and demands that Satan leave his presence. This last temptation is absurd and gets little or no consideration. However, Jesus has endured a severe attack by the ruler of death and evil and needs to be administered by the angels.

There are millions of angels that minister to children on a daily basis in many different ways. They will provide direction to children by speaking to them in a way they will understand, they may distract them long enough to avoid a dangerous situation, or in some cases actually work through another person to change their living situation. Guardian angels are an important part of the everyday life of the believer. They know what is in the future and will guide us through different situations. We need to remember that we are under constant review by the angels and we need to live our life in a way that would not be offensive to them. Acts 27:23 reads, For there stood by me this night the angel of God, whose I am, and whom I serve. Guarding angels may come to a child in pairs just as Jesus sent the disciples out in pairs. The first angel will provide great comfort in holding the child until they are at peace. Psalm 91:4, reads, He shall cover thee with his feathers, and under his wings shalt thou trust: his truth shall be thy shield and buckler. This comfort is not what we normally associate with a physical feeling, but with all encompassing warmth that brings the spirit and body at peace and may prepare the child for a second angel. Luke 2:13 reads, And suddenly there was with the angel a multitude of the heavenly host praising God, and saying. If needed a second angel may actually speak with force and pull the child to safety. Again, this is not a voice you hear with your ears and feel the pull on your body.

The angel Gabriel was a messenger that often delivered information to those in need. The angel Gabriel would provide assurance to those he approached with a word of peace and safety.

Luke 1:19 reads, And the angel answering said unto him, I am Gabriel, that stand in the presence of God; and am sent to speak unto thee, and to show thee these glad tidings.

The angel Gabriel delivered a message to Zechariah that his prayers were heard and that his wife Elisabeth would bear a son.

Luke 1:26-38 reads, And in the sixth month the angel Gabriel was sent from God unto the city of Galilee, named Nazareth. To a virgin espoused to a man whose name was Joseph, of the house of David; and the virgin's name was Mary. And the angel came in unto her, and said, Hail, thou that art highly favored, the Lord is with thee: blessed art thou among women. And when she was him, she was troubled at his saying, and cast in her mind what manner of salutation this should be. And the angel said unto her, Fear not, Mary: for thou hast found favor with God. And, behold, thou shalt conceive in thy womb, and bring forth a son, and shall call his name JESUS. He shall be great, and shall be called the Son of the Highest: and the Lord God shall give unto him the throne of his father David. And he shall reign over the house of Jacob for ever: and his kingdom there shall be no end. Then said Mary unto the angel, How shall this be, seeing I know not a man. And the angel answered and said unto her, The Holy Ghost shall come upon thee, and the power of the Highest shall overshadow thee: therefore also that holy thing which shall be born of thee shall be called the Son of God. And, behold, thy cousin Elizabeth, she hath also conceived a son in her old age: and this is the sixth month with her, who was called barren. For with God nothing shall be impossible. And Mary said, Behold the handmaid of the Lord; be it unto me according to thy word. And the angle departed from her.

The angel Gabriel delivered a message to Mary and remained with her for a period of time to explain what was about to transpire. She was chosen by God to deliver to this earth the Son of God for the salvation of all mankind.

1 Corinthians 4:9 reads, For I think that God hath set forth us the apostles last, as it were appointed to death: for we are made a spectacle unto the world, and to angels, and to men.

Our lives are a spectacle to all the angels and the principalities.

Satan attacks again and again regardless of the outcome. Satan is an extremely powerful supernatural fallen angel capable of transporting Jesus from the wilderness to the Temple in Jerusalem to the highest mountains in Israel. In another supernatural act Satan was able to show Jesus the kingdoms of the world and without consideration for the truth offers these kingdoms to Jesus for his rule. Satan is extremely cunning and knows our weaknesses and will attack us with his demons when we are the most vulnerable. These attacks can come in many different forms and from many different sources.

We see these acts of pure evil each day as man drifts deeper into social decay and people are no longer able discern good from evil. What was considered illegal and not appropriate for public discussion fifty years ago is now on display for a child's viewing. The basic social values have been eroded to the point where even the definition of a family is no longer understood.

The First Recorded Miracles by Jesus Were in Galilee

Changing water into wine

JOHN 2: 11 READS, The beginning of miracles did Jesus in Cana of Galilee, and manifested forth his glory: and his disciples believed on him.

The purpose of this first recorded miracle was to reveal the glory of Jesus the Savior and that a spiritual transformation had taken place. This miracle occurred before Jesus began his ministry and occurred at a wedding with his mother Mary and his disciples. The miracle involved changing water into wine due to the fact they ran out of wine during the wedding celebration.

John 2: 3-8 reads, And when they wanted wine the mother of Jesus saith unto him, they have no wine. Jesus saith unto her, "Woman, what have I to do with thee? Mine hour is not yet come." His mother said unto the servants, Whatsoever he saith unto you, do it. And there were set there six waterpots of stone, after the manner of the purifying of the Jews, containing two or three firkins apiece. Jesus saith unto them, "Fill the waterpots with water.' And they filled them up to the brim. And he saith unto them, "Draw out now, and bear unto the governor of the feast." And they did so.

The relationship between Mary and Jesus is changing as Jesus begins his ministry. Obviously, Mary knew who Jesus was and that He could easily transform the water into wine. However, at this time Jesus begins to instruct Mary his mother that his ministry will determine when miracles will be accomplished. After the wedding, Jesus travels to Capernaum (located on the northern shore of the Sea of Galilee) with his mother, brothers and disciples.

Jesus then travels to Jerusalem for the Passover and drives out the money changers from the temple. After which, He along with His disciples travel to the Judea country side and the disciples begin to baptize new believers. They continue their travels northward through the territory of Samaria where he asks a Samaritan woman for drink from a well. The Samaritans were hated by the Jews due to their mixed society and rejection of the Old Testament. Consequently, Jesus speaking to this woman would be met with great distain by most Jews. Jesus early in his ministry is saying He does not recognize Jewish opinions or their attitudes towards people. He did not judge the Samaritan woman, but guided and instructed her how she could follow a path to righteousness. He is willing and open to share the gospel with all men regardless of their status in life and their past history. This introduces Jesus' ministry to Samaria where many people becomes believers. They eventually return to Cana of Galilee where He heals an officer's son that was located in Capernaum.

Healing of the Nobleman's son

A nobleman came to Cana to beg Jesus to save his son because he was gravely ill.

John 4: 46-50 reads, So Jesus came again into Cana of Galilee, where he made the water wine. And there was a certain nobleman, whose son was sick at Capernaum. When he heard that Jesus was come out of Judea into Galilee, he went unto him, and besought him that he would come down, and heal his son: for he was at the point of death. Then said Jesus unto him, "Except ye see signs and wonders, ye will not believe." The nobleman saith unto him, Sir, come down ere my child die. Jesus saith unto him, "Go thy way: thy son liveth." And the man believed the word that Jesus had spoken unto him, and he went his way.

The nobleman took Jesus at his word and believed his son would be healed from the illness. This belief without question by the nobleman was directly responsible for the son being healed. The lesson to be learned is that we need to develop a belief that is without doubt, without hesitation, and is able to withstand the severest of tests. Developing that type of faith requires us to receive Christ and to follow God and the Holy Spirits direction. Growth requires work and time on the part of believers through study of the Bible, prayer, confession, profession, and persistence.

Galatians 3:22 reads, But the scripture hath concluded all under sin, that the promise by faith of Jesus Christ might be given to them that believe. But before faith came, we were kept under the law, shut up unto the faith which should afterwards be revealed. Wherefore the law was our schoolmaster to bring us unto Christ, that we might be justified by faith. But after that faith is come, we are no longer under the schoolmaster. For ye are all the children of God by faith in Christ Jesus. For as many of you as have been baptized into Christ have put on Christ.

Jesus returns to his home town Nazareth and then moves back to Capernaum where he presses his disciples into full time service. While in Capernaum and teaching in a synagogue He heals a man possessed by demons.

The Approximate Beginning of Jesus' Second Year of Ministry

THE SECOND YEAR OF Jesus' ministry is generally spent around the northern part of the Sea of Galilee. He moves to Capernaum and travels throughout the local area except for a trip to Jerusalem. He also continues to select disciples during this time period. During this time period he is healing and preaching and is continually training his disciples. Jesus in many cases teaches his disciples by example when healing and speaking to those that are suffering from many different types of afflictions. He teaches His disciples by showing love and mercy for those that are in need. He is not a respecter of wealth or status, but looks straight into their spirit to determine if they have faith, love, hope and charity. He is looking for a spirit that will be receptive to God's word and will love God and show His love to their neighbors.

Healing of a man with a demon

Jesus was preaching in a synagogue on the Sabbath in Capernaum when a man began shouting at Jesus. The man was possessed by a demon and could not control himself. Jesus healed this man and the news of the healing quickly spread throughout the area.

Mark 1:21-28 reads, And they went into Capernaum: and straightway on the Sabbath day he entered into the synagogue, and taught. And they were astonished at his doctrine: for he taught them as one that had authority, and not as the scribes. And there was in their synagogue a man with an unclean spirit: and he cried out. Saying let us alone; what have we to do with thee, thou Jesus of Nazareth? Art thou come to destroy us? I know thee who thou art, the Holy One of God. And Jesus rebuked him, saying, "Hold thy peace, and come out of him." And when the unclean spirit had torn him, and cried with a loud voice, he came out of him.

When Jesus speaks the words "Hold thy peace" the unclean spirit is held and then removed from this man in torment. We see today that people who are completely consumed by their own greed will begin to convulse when they hear God's word. They recognize God's word and are quick to react asking to be left alone. The demons of today are no different than the demons that Jesus drove from this poor man.

Healing of Simon's (Peter) mother-in-law and others

After leaving the synagogue Jesus and the disciples went to Simon's (Peter) home. There they met Peter's mother-in-law who was suffering from a high fever and there they asked Jesus to help her.

Luke 4:38-39 reads, And he arose out of the synagogue, and entered into Simon's house. And Simon's wife's mother was taken with a great fever: and they besought him for her. And he stood over her, and rebuked the fever; and it left her and immediately she arose and ministered unto them.

Many more people were then brought to Jesus that day for the healing of different health issues. The sun was setting and it was now appropriate to carry the sick.

Luke 4:40-41 reads, Now when the sun was setting, all they that had any sick with drivers disease brought them unto him; and he laid his hands on every one of them, and healed them. And devils also came out of many, crying out, and saying, Thou art Christ the Son of God. And he rebuking them suffered them not to speak: for they knew that he was Christ.

The word spread quickly that Jesus was able the heal people of many different affirmatives. Jesus was the example of one who loves his neighbor and is willing help those in need. However, Jesus wanted to focus on his primary mission to redeem sinners from death and not allow the healing to take away from his mission.

Miracle at Sea of Galilee

Jesus instructs Peter to move the boat out further into the lake to catch more fish. Peter explains they have been fishing all night and have not caught any fish. But, he now follows Jesus' direction regardless of what he has experienced and moves the boat and lets down the nets. Peter, an expert fisherman, has not allowed his pride to take control of his words and actions, but takes instruction from Jesus. Pride, arrogance, and ego will block communication with the Holy Spirit and will prevent blessings from taking place in our life and those around us.

Luke 5:3-10 reads, And he entered into one of the ships, which was Simon's and prayed him that he would thrust out a little from the land. And he sat down, and taught the people, and taught the people out of the ship. Now when he had left speaking, he said unto Simon, "Launch out into the deep, and let down your nets for a draught." And Simon answering said unto him, Master, we have toiled all the night, and have taken nothing: nevertheless at thy word I will let down the net. And when they had this done, they enclosed a great multitude of fishes: and their net brake. And they beckoned unto their partners, which were in the other ship, that they should come and help them. And they came, and filled both ships, so that they began to sink. When Simon Peter saw it, he fell down at Jesus' knees, saying, Depart from me; for I am a sinful man, O Lord. For he was astonished, and all that were with him, at the daught of the fishes which they had taken. And so was also James, and John, the sons of Zebedee, which were partners with Simon. And Jesus said unto Simon, "Fear not; from henceforth thou shalt catch men."

Peter and his partners (James and John) were astonished by the number of fish they caught and realized this was beyond their skills as fishermen. They also realized that Jesus had a divine nature and their lives were sinful and they felt unworthy to be in the presence of Jesus.

Jesus begins again His travels throughout Galilee preaching and healing. These healings include healing lepers, a Roman centurion's servant, a man paralyzed, a man with a shriveled hand, raising a widows' son from the dead, and healing a man demon-possessed in Gadarene.

Healing a man with Leprosy

A leper approached Jesus while he was returning from teaching.

Mark 1: 40-45 reads, And there came a leper to him, beseeching him, and kneeling down to him, and saying unto him, If thou wilt thou canst make me clean. And Jesus, moved with compassion, put forth his hand, and touched him, and saith unto him, "I will be thou clean." And as soon as he had spoken, immediately the leprosy departed from him, and he was cleansed. And he straitly charged him, and forthwith sent him away. And saith unto him, "See thou say nothing to any man: but go thy way, show thyself to the priest, and offer for thy cleaning those things which Moses commanded, for a testimony unto them." But he went out, and began to publish it much, and to blaze abroad the matter, insomuch that Jesus could no more openly enter into the city, but was without in desert places: and they came to him from every quarter.

News of this healing began to get a great deal of attention and Jesus had to move to a remote area. However, people continued to search for him from many different areas throughout the countryside.

Healing a centurion's servant

A centurion, a Roman soldier that had authority over many soldiers had a servant that was sick and about to die. The centurion was a man that felt he was not worthy of Jesus' attention and asked that Jesus only speak of his servant to be healed.

Matthew 8:5-13 reads, And when Jesus was entered into Capernaum, there came unto him a centurion, beseeching him, And saying, lord, my servant lieth at home sick of the palsy, grievously tormented. And Jesus saith unto him, "I will come and heal him." The centurion answered and said, Lord I am not worthy that thou shouldest come under my roof: but speak the word only, and my servant shall be healed. For I am a man under authority, having soldiers under me: and I say to this man, Go, and he goeth: and to another come, and he cometh; and to my servant, Do this, and he doeth it. When Jesus heard it, he marveled, and said to them that followed, "Verily I say unto you, I have not found so great faith, no, not in Israel. And I say unto you, that many shall come from the east and west, and shall sit down with Abraham, and Isaac, and Jacob, in the kingdom of heaven. But the children of the kingdom shall be cast out into outer darkness: there shall be weeping and gnashing of teeth." And Jesus said unto the centurion, "Go they way: and as thou hast believed, so be it done unto thee." And his servant was healed in the selfsame hour.

The centurion's strong faith in Jesus' divine power resulted in the servant being healed without the presence of Jesus at his side. In this situation it was the faith of a Gentile that lead to the healing of this servant. Jesus also proclaims that many will come from the east and west (Gentiles) and shall sit down with Abraham, and Isaac, and Jacob, in the Kingdom of heaven. Jesus' message was for all of mankind regardless of what they were, where they were in society, or what they did in the past.

I John 5: 2-5 reads, By this we know that we love the children of God, when we love God, and keep his commandments. For this is the love of God, that we keep his commandments: and his commandments are not grievous. For whatsoever is born of God overcometh the world: and this is the victory that overcometh the world, even our faith. Who is he that overcometh the world, but he that believeth that Jesus is the Son of God.

Healing a paralyzed man

By this time Jesus was attracting large crowds of people where ever he went. In this situation, there were some men who could not get a paralyzed man on a mat past the crowds that surrounded Jesus. In an act of desperation these men carried this paralyzed man onto the roof of the house and made an opening in the roof to lower him down for Jesus to see.

Mark 2:3-12 reads, And they come unto him, bringing one sick of the palsy, which was borne of four. And when they could not come nigh unto him for the press, they uncovered the roof where he was, and when they had broken it up, they let down the bed wherein the sick of the palsy lay. When Jesus saw their faith, he said unto the sick of the palsy, "Son, thy sins be forgiven thee." But there were certain of the scribes sitting there, and reasoning in their hearts. Why doth this man thus speak blasphemies? Who can forgive sin but God only? And immediately when Jesus perceived in his spirit that they so reasoned within themselves, he said unto them, "Why reason ye these things in your hearts?" "Whether is it easier to say to the sick of the palsy, Thy sins be forgiven thee: or to say, Arise, and take up thy bed, and walk." "But that ye may know that the Son of man hath power on earth to forgive sins." (he saith to the sick of the palsy.) "I say unto thee, Arise, and take up thy bed, and go thy way unto thine house." And immediately he arose, and went forth before them all; insomuch that they were all amazed, and glorified God, saying, we never saw it in this fashion.

Romans 5:12 reads, Wherefore, as by one man sin entered into the world, and death by sin; and so death passed upon all men, for that all have sinned.

Sin entered into the world with Adam and Eve. This resulted in man being infected with many diseases that has caused great sorrow for many people for many years. In this case, Jesus said, (Mark 2:5), "Son, thy sins be forgiven thee." By saying this and healing this man Jesus connected sin with the frailty of man and the resulting death.

We need to remember that Satan and his demons lurk in the darkness and have authority over death, disease, and sin. As the world sinks deeper into sin, death and disease will follow.

Healing a withered hand

This miracle was completed in a Synagogue on the Sabbath and was used by the Pharisees to plot against Jesus.

Mark 3:3-6 reads, And he saith unto the man which had a withered hand, "Stand forth." And he saith unto them, "Is it lawful to do good on the Sabbath days, or to do evil? To save life or to kill?" But they held their peace. And when he looked round about on them with anger, being grieved for the hardness of their hearts, he saith unto the man, "Stretch forth thine hand". And he stretch it out: and his hand was restored whole as the other. And the Pharisees went forth, and straightway took counsel with the Herodians against him, how they might destroy him.

Jesus is saying to meet this man's needs on the Sabbath is to do good, to fail to meet this man's needs would be evil.

The Pharisees consulted with the Herodians in trying to discredit Jesus. They were political opportunist and saw Jesus as a threat to Roman rule. Consequently, they were trying to use Jewish tradition or Roman law as a tool to discredit Jesus.

1 Timothy 6:11 reads, But thou, O man of God, flee these things; and follow after righteousness, godliness, faith, love, patience, meekness.

Roman 1:17 reads, For therein is the righteousness of God revealed from faith to faith, as it is written, THE JUST SHALL LIVE BY FAITH.

Raising a widow's son

Jesus was traveling to the town of Nain with a large crowd of people. As they approached the city they met a funeral procession. There was a widow with a group of people carrying a dead child.

Luke 7: 11-17 reads, And it came to pass the day after, that he went into a city called Nain; and many of his disciples went with him, and much people. Now when he came night to the gate of the city, behold, there was a dead man carried out, the only son of his mother, and she was a widow: and much people of the city was with her. And when the Lord saw her, he had compassion on her, and said unto her, "Weep not." And he came and touched the bier (open coffin), and they that bare him stood still. And he said, "Young man, I say unto thee, Arise." And he that was dead sat up, and began to speak. And he delivered him to his mother. And there came a fear on all, and they glorified God, saying, That a great prophet is risen up among us; and That God hath visited his people. And this rumor of him went forth throughout all Judea, and throughout all the region round about.

Jesus took compassion on this widow as she wept over the loss of her only son. He gave this young man back his life so that he may comfort his mother and to provide for her. The magnitude of this miracle made people realize that they were in the presence of a great prophet. Again, Jesus's reputation grew as more and more people heard of the miracles.

1 Peter 3:8 reads, Finally, be ye all of one mind, having compassion one of another, love as brethren, be pitiful, be courteous.

Ephesians 3:19-21 reads, And to know the love of Christ, which passeth knowledge that ye might be filled with all the fullness of God. Now unto him that is able to do exceeding abundantly above all that we ask or think, according to the power that worketh in us. Unto him be glory in the church by Christ Jesus throughout all ages, world without end. Amen.

Calming the storm

It was not unusual for storms to develop on the Sea of Galilee. However, this was an exceptionally strong storm that threatened to capsize the boat.

Mark 4:35-41 reads, And the same day, when the even was come, he saith unto them, "Let us pass over unto the other side."

And when they had sent away the multitude, they took him even as he was in the ship. And there were with him other little ships. And there arose a great storm of wind, and the waves beat into the ship, so that it was now full. And he was in the hinder part of the ship, asleep on a pillow: and they awake him, and say unto him, Master, carest thou not that we parish? And he arose, and rebuked the wind, and said unto the sea, "Peace, be still". And the wind ceased, and there was a great calm. And he said unto them, "Why are ye so fearful? How is it that ye have no faith?" And they feared exceedingly, and said one to another, What manner of man is this, that even the wind and the sea obey him?

Only God has the power to calm the seas and silence the wind. Psalm 107: 29 reads, He maketh the storm a calm, so that the waves thereof are still. Jesus' presence and his power over the wind and sea bolstered the faith of his disciples.

Galatians 3:22 reads, But the scripture hath concluded all under sin, that the promise by faith of Jesus Christ might be given to them that believe.

Healing the Gerasene man

After reaching the other side of the Sea of Galilee they landed in an area called Gerasene and there they met a man possessed by demons. He was a strong man that could break the chains that were used to try to restrain him. He roamed this area at night crying out from the tombs and cutting himself. When he saw Jesus, he ran to him and fell on his knees.

Mark 5: 2-3 reads, And when he was come out of the ship. Immediately there met him out of the tombs a man with an unclean spirit. Who had his dwelling among the tombs: and no man could bind him, no, not with chains.

Mark 5: 6-13 reads, But when he saw Jesus afar off, he ran and worshiped him. And cried with aloud voice, and said, What have I to do with thee, Jesus, thou Son of the most high God? I adjure thee by God, that thou torment me not. For he said unto him, "Come out of the man, thou unclean spirit." And he asked him,

"What is thy name?" And he answered, saying, My name is Legion: for we are many. And he besought him much that he would not send them away out of the country. Now there was there nigh unto the mountains a great herd of swine feeding. And all the devils besought him, saying, Send us into the swine, that we may enter into them. And forthwith Jesus gave them leave. And the unclean spirit went out, and entered into the swine: and the herd ran violently down a steep place into the sea, (they were about two thousand ;) and were choked in the sea.

This man was able to recognize that Jesus was God. This was possible because the demonic powers within this man knew the true identity of Christ. The demon that spoke was named Legion because there were many demons that possessed this man. A Legion is 6,000 in the Roman army.

Jesus spoke with one of the demons as he commanded him come out of this poor man's body. The demons had been tormenting this poor man to the point of driving this man to insanity. After being freed from these demons, this man wanted to remain with Jesus.

Jesus took mercy on this man and delivered him from his bondage and requested that he return to his people to give testimony of what God had done in his life. God provides blessings in each of our lives for the primary propose of us testifying to others of his love and his continued presence.

Society refuses to recognize the existence of demons and the church profoundly underestimates the power of demons. We see the existence of these demons on a daily basis as children are killed by young men and women fighting on the streets over drugs. We see a world consumed with greed with no thought or concern for the poor.

1 John 5:5 reads, Who is he that overcometh the world, but he that believeth that Jesus is the Son of God.

Healing a woman with internal bleeding

A woman with great faith was healed of her internal bleeding issue simply by touching the clothes of Jesus.

Mark 5: 25-34 reads, And a certain women, which had an issue of blood twelve years. And had suffered many things of many physicians, and had spent all that she had, and was nothing bettered, but rather grew worse. When she had heard of Jesus, came in the press behind, and touched his garment. For she said, If I may touch but his clothes, I shall be whole. And straightway the fountain of her blood was dried up; and she felt in her body that she was healed of that plague. And Jesus, immediately knowing in himself that virtue had gone out of him, turned him about in the press, and said, "Who touched my clothes".

In this case, Jesus recognized this touch of faith and allowed this women to be healed of her condition. This is another example of where faith and knowledge of God's presence in our daily life allows us to reach out to touch his word and know he will provide for our needs. The will of God to bless us is always there along with human need, suffering, and sinfulness. Faith is the component that allows His blessing to resolve issues and situations that are beyond our control and comprehension.

Hebrews 1:3 reads, Who being the brightness of his glory, and the express image of his person, and upholding all things by the word of his power, when he had by himself purged our sins, sat down on the right hand of the Majesty on high.

Jesus was equal to the Father and his brightness was the shining of his divine glory. His power was without question and all things are possible to those who believe.

Raising Jairus' daughter

Jairus was a synagogue leader who was pleading with Jesus to come to his house because his daughter was dying. As with many other people during this period of time, Jairus' daughter was facing a life and death situation due to disease and other related health issues.

Jesus was being pulled in many directions because so many people were suffering from many different health issues.

Mark 5: 35-43 reads, While he yet spake, there came from the ruler of the synagogue's house certain which said, Thy daughter is dead: why troublest thou the Master any further. As soon as Jesus heard the word that was spoken, he saith unto the ruler of the synagogue, "Be not afraid, only believe." And he suffered no man to follow him, save Peter, and James, and John the brother of James. And he cometh to the house of the ruler of the synagogue, and seeth the trumult, and them that wept and wailed greatly. And when he was come in, he saith unto them, "Why make ye this ado, and weep? The damsel is not dead, but sleepeth." And they laughed him to scorn. But when he had put them all out, he taketh the father and mother of the damsel, and them that were with him, and entereth in where the damsel was lying. And he took the damsel by the hand, and said unto her, "Talitha cumi"; which is, being interpreted, "Damsel" (I say unto thee) "arise". And straightway the damsel arose, and walked; for she was of age of twelve years. And they were astonished with a great astonishment. And he charged them straitly that no man should know it; and commanded that something should be given her to eat.

In this case, Jesus tells Jairus not to be afraid and only to believe. He wants Jairus to focus on the fact that God is in control and not to waste time worrying, but to pray. Secondly, Jesus requires that non- believers be removed from the home. He does not want the mourners and the syndical laughter to be a distraction. At this point, Jairus, his wife, Peter, James, John the brother of James and Jesus are in the room with the daughter. Jesus takes the hand of the girl and said, "Taliths cumi" (Little girl arise). Without hesitation the twelve year old got up from the bed and began walking. Jairus and his wife were naturally amazed and overwhelmed with joy that their daughter was alive. Again, Jesus commanded the parents not to tell of the miracle because of the crisis that would be created by the Jewish and government leadership.

Mark 11:24 reads, "Therefore I say unto you, What things soever ye desire, when ye pray, believe that ye receive them, and ye shall have them."

We need to remember to bring all of our needs before God in prayer and to rejoice in thanksgiving for all of our blessings on a daily basis. Acknowledge what God has done and praise his name for the greatest of gift His Son.

The Approximate Beginning of the Third Year of Jesus' Ministry

IT APPEARS THE MAJOR portion of the recorded miracles occurred during the third and final year of Jesus' ministry here on earth. During this final year Jesus travels great distances from the northern part of Israel down to the Dead Sea area and Jerusalem. He is rejected for the second time in Nazareth and sends out his twelve disciples to preach the Gospel. Jesus and His disciples return to Capernaum and later travel by boat to Bethsaida where Jesus feeds 5,000 people. They again travel by boat in the Sea of Galilee to the plain of Gannesaret where many people are healed. Even as the time grows short and before Jesus is lead to His death, He continues to show mercy with healings and revealing His never ending love for His people. He also raises Lazarus who had been dead for four days. In fact, as Jesus travels through Jericho to Jerusalem He heals Bartimeus of blindness only days before His crucifixion. His love and mercy knows no boundary.

Healing two blind men

The reputation of Jesus' power to heal was rapidly spreading across the country to the point where people are seeking him out. In this situation two blind men were following him calling out for mercy.

Matthew 9: 27-31 reads, And when Jesus departed thence, two blind men followed him crying, and saying, Thou son of David, have mercy on us. And when he was come into the house, the blind men came to him: and Jesus saith unto them, "Believe ye that I am able to do this?' They said unto him, Yea Lord. Then touched he their eyes, saying, "According to your faith be it unto you." And their eyes were opened: and Jesus strictly charged them, saying, "See that no man know it." But they, when they were departed, spread abroad his fame in all that country.

As with other miracles, Jesus required that these men be separated from the crowd and be allowed to follow him into a house. These men also cried out, Thou son of David, and called Jesus Lord. Their willingness to acknowledge Jesus as Lord and their faith in his ability was responsible for the healing of their blindness.

There should be no hesitation in acknowledging God's continued blessings and His love for us.

Proverbs 3:5-6 reads, Trust in the lord with all thine heart; and lean not unto thine own understanding. In all thine ways acknowledge him, and he shall direct thy paths.

Healing a mute demon-possessed

At this point, Jesus is being confronted by many people some with infirmities that they have lived with for many years. Again, Jesus shows mercy.

Matthew 9:32-33 reads, And they went out, behold, they brought to him a dumb man possessed with a devil. And when the devil was cast out, the dumb spake: and the multitudes marveled, saying, It was never so seen in Israel.

One can sense the turmoil that is being created as more miracles were performed and the crowds were growing larger. Matthew does not give a lot of detail, but he does use the word multitude to give an idea of the size of crowds. Again, we are made aware of the demonic presence of that day and their effect on the common man.

Healing a man who was crippled

Jesus heals a man who was cripped for 38 years. This man was laying besides the pool of Bethesda in Jerusalem, a place where people came in the hope of being healed.

John 5: 1-12 reads, After this there was a feast of the Jews: and Jesus went up to Jerusalem. Now there is at Jerusalem by the sheep market a pool, which is called in the Hebrew tongue Bethesda, having five porches. In these lay a great multitude of impotent folk, of blind, halt, withered, waiting for the moving of the water. For an angel went down at a certain season into the pool, and troubled the water: whosoever then first after the troubling of the water stepped in was made whole of whatsoever disease he had. And a certain man was there, which had an infirmity thirty and eight years. When Jesus saw him lie, and knew that he had been now a long time in that case, he saith unto him, "Wilt thou be made whole." The impotent man answered him, Sir, I have no man, when the water is troubled, to put me into the pool: but while I am coming, another steppeth down before me. Jesus saith unto him, "Rise take up thy bed, and walk." And immediately the man was made whole, and took up his bed, and walked: and on the same day was the Sabbath.

The Jewish authorities found out that Jesus healed this man on the Sabbath and were wroth with anger and were looking to kill him. Jesus also said that God was his Father and that even further enraged the Jewish authorities.

It is at approximately this time that Jesus provides an explanation of his deity to the Jews. They have been looking to persecute him for healing people on the Sabbath day. The Pharisees had added many traditions to the law that prevented any type of burden to be performed on the Sabbath. Jesus explains that He is God and that He does not answer to man for His acts of compassion and mercy.

John 5:19-23 reads, Then answered Jesus and said unto them, "Verily, verily, I say unto you, The Son can do nothing of himself, but what he seeth the Father do: for what things soever he doeth, these also doeth the Son likewise. For the Father loveth the

Son, and showeth him all things that himself doeth: and he will show him greater works than these, that ye may marvel. For as the Father judgeth no man, but hath committed all judgment unto the Son. That all men should honor the Son, even as they honor the Father. He that honoreth not the Son honoreth not the Father which hath sent him."

Jesus explains that God is his Father and that He is equal to his Father. The Pharisees consider this explanation as blasphemy that is subject to death. Jesus has forced the Pharisees to either recognize Jesus as their God that has the authority to show compassion and mercy on the Sabbath or to condemn Him as a heretic.

John 10:35-38 reads, "If he called them Gods, unto whom the word of God came, and the scripture cannot be broken. Say ye of him, whom the Father hath sanctified, and sent into the world, Thou blasphemest; because I said, I am the Son of God. If I do not the works of my Father, believe me not. But if I do, though ye believe not me, believe the works: that ye may know, and believe, that the Father is in me, and I in him."

Jesus was obedient to the Father in showing mercy by healing those in need. The Jewish authorities had to recognize the fact that Jesus was a doer of the word and was showing mercy that is found in the Old Testaments (Deut. 25-4). We need to be careful that we are not only hearers, but also doers of the word.

Feeding 5000 men and their families

At this time many people were following Jesus and his disciples and it was getting more difficult to escape the crowds. Jesus again took mercy on these people and realized they were like sheep looking for a shepherd. He fed them and began to explain the message of salvation.

Mark 6: 35-44 reads, And when the day was now far spent, his disciples came unto him, and said, This is a desert place, and now the time is far passed. Send them away, that they may go into the country round about, and into the villages, and buy themselves bread: for they have nothing to eat. He answered and said unto them, "Give ye them to eat." And they say unto him, Shall we go and buy two hundred pennyworth of bread, and give them to eat? He saith unto them, "How many loaves have ye? go and see." And when they knew, they say Five, and two fishes. And he commanded them to make all sit down by companies upon the green grass. And they sat down in ranks, by hundreds, and by fifties. And when he had taken the five loaves and the two fishes, he looked up to heaven, and blessed and brake the loaves, and gave them to his disciples to set before them; and the two fishes divided he among them all. And they did all eat, and were filled. And they took up twelve baskets full of the fragments, and of the fishes. And they that did eat of the loaves were about five thousand men.

Capernaum and other towns in the area would only have about two to three hundred inhabitants. So this crowd of five thousand men (not including women and children) would be immense in comparison.

As with other miracles, Jesus gathered his disciples together and prayed that God's grace would provide a miracle that would meet the needs for his people. Jesus also took the bread and broke it so as to divide it so that all who were in need would be filled.

John 14:12-14 reads, "Verily, verily, I say unto you, He that believeth on me, the works that I do shall he do also; and greater works than these shall he do; because I go unto my Father. And whatsoever ye shall ask in my name, that will I do, that the Father may be glorified in the Son. If ye shall ask anything in my name, I will do it."

Our prayers are to be both in union and in the will of our Father. We are to ask for all things in His name so that all blessings are received in thanksgiving and glorifying His name. Free will allows us to have a faith that provides freedom for us to experience His blessings.

Walking on water

After dismissing the crowd of 5000 men, Jesus departed and went up into the mountains to pray. Jesus was still training his disciples and he knew there was still work to be done. That evening Jesus asked his disciples to sail to other side of the sea of Galilee.

Mark 6:45-50 reads, And straightway he constrained his disciples to get into the ship, and go to the other side before Bethsaida, while he sent away the people. And when he had sent them away, he departed into the mountain to pray. And when even was come, the ship was in the midst of the sea, and he alone on the land. And he saw them toiling in rowing: for the wind was contrary unto them: and about the fourth watch of the night he cometh unto them, walking upon the sea, and would have passed by them. But when they all saw him walking upon the sea, supposed it had been a spirit, and cried out. For they all saw him, and were troubled. And immediately he talked with them, and saith unto them, "Be of good cheer: it is I; be not afraid."

It was about three or four in the morning and the disciples were struggling from rolling against the sea and the wind. They were exhausted and out of the darkness appeared a figure walking on the water. The disciples were terrorized thinking they were seeing a spirit approaching them. Jesus called out to them and entered the boat to reassure them that it was He and immediately the wind ceased. The disciples needed to understand that Jesus had authority over the wind and the sea and that he was continually demonstrating His deity.

By this time Jesus' reputation had grown to the point where many people were looking for him to relieve them of their many affirmatives. Some people were saying that Jesus should be king. All of this activity would have gotten the attention of Jewish leadership and the Roman leaders in Jerusalem.

The Healing of many at Gennesaret

Once Jesus and disciples landed on shore at Gennesaret they were recognized and word of their arrival quickly spread throughout the area. People were running with the sick on mats trying to get Jesus' attention and blessings.

Mark 6:53-56 reads, And when they had passed over, they came into the land of Gennesaret, and drew to the shore. And when they were come out of the ship, straightway they knew him. And ran throughout that whole region round about, and began to carry about beds those that were sick, where they heard he was. And whithsoever he entered, into villages, or cities, or country, they laid the sick in the streets, and besought him that they might touch if it were but the border of his garment: and as many as touched him were made whole.

This is the second time in the Gospel of Mark where people were being healed simply by touching Christ's garment. We are told that as many touched him were made whole. The number of those that were healed was great considering the mention of villages, cities, and the countryside. God took mercy on the sick and those that were in need.

Psalm 103:11 reads, For as the heaven is high above the earth, so great is his mercy toward them that fear him.

Psalm 105: 1-3 reads, O give thanks unto the Lord; call upon his name: make know his deeds among the people. Sing unto him, sing psalms unto him: talk ye of all his wondrous works. Glory ye in his holy name, let the heart of them rejoice that seek the Lord.

The Lord provided for the Israelites in many ways over the years. He guided them from Egypt and provided for them in the wilderness. God's blessings are beyond our comprehension. Therefore, everyone is required to praise His name and rejoice in His unconditional love.

Healing a girl possessed by a demon

Jesus then left the Gennesaret area and moved to the area of Tyre and Sidon. When he arrived he was met by a Canaanite women who asked Jesus to heal her daughter of demon-possession.

Mark 7:24-30 reads, And from thence he arose, and went into the borders of Tyre and Sidon, and entered into a house, and would have no man know it: but he could not be hid. For a certain woman, whose young daughter had an unclean spirit, heard of him, and came and fell at his feet. The woman was a Greek a Syrophoenician by nation, and she besought him that he would cast forth the devil out of her daughter. But Jesus said unto her, " Let the children first be filled: for it is not meet to take the children's bread, and to cast it unto the dogs". And she answered and said unto him, Yes, lord: yet the dogs under the table eat the children's crumbs. And he said unto her, "For this saying go thy way: the devil is gone out of thy daughter". And when she was come to her house, she found the devil gone out, and her daughter laid upon the bed.

Jesus and the disciples were tired and were looking for a place for instruction when they entered into this Gentile territory. A woman approached Jesus and called Him Son of David because she realized he must be the Messiah. This woman was persistent and had great faith in Jesus and was able to respond to Jesus with the understanding that Gentiles were in need of salvation. This miracle was performed at a distance and without any recorded command by Jesus.

1 Corinthians 13:1 reads, Though I speak with the tongues of men and of angels, and have not charity, I am become as sounding brass, or a tinkling cymbal.

Jesus again shows that charity and compassion takes priority in all situations. Jesus focus is to teach us that love for our neighbor is paramount.

Healing of a deaf man

Jesus left the Tyre area and went down to the Sea of Galilee into the region of Decapolis. There He was approached by people asking that He heal a man who was deaf and had problems speaking.

Mark 7:31-37 reads, And again, departing from the coasts of Tyre and Sidon, he came near to the Sea of Galilee, through the midst of the coasts of Decapolis. And they bring unto him one that was deaf, and had an impediment in his speech; and they beseech him to put his hand upon him. And they took him aside from the multitude, and put his fingers unto his ears, and he spit, and touched his tongue. And looking up to the heaven, he sighed, and saith unto him, "Ephphatha", that is, "He opened". And straightway his ears were open, and the string of his tongue was loosed, and he spake plain. And he charged them that they should tell no man; but the more he charged them, so much the more a great deal they published it. And were beyond measure astonished, saying, he hath done all things well: he maketh both the deaf to hear, and dumb to speak.

Again, large crowds of people were following Jesus and asking Him to heal people as He moved along the eastern shores of Galilee. Jesus asked that they tell no one of these miracles, but the crowds continue to spread the word of these miracles.

1 John 4:10 reads, Herein is love, not that we loved God, but that he loved us, and spent his Son to be the propitiation for our sins.

1 John 4:20 reads, If a man say, I love God, and hateth his brother, he is a liar: for he that loveth not his brother whom he hath seen, how can he love God whom he hath not seen.

God's love for all mankind is unconditional. The decision to accept or reject this love is entirely up to each individual.

Romans 10:9 reads, That if thou shalt confess with thy mouth the Lord Jesus, and shalt believe in thine heart that God hath raised him from the dead, thou shalt be saved.

Deuteronomy 30:10-14 reads, If thou shalt hearken unto the voice of the Lord thy God, to keep his commandments and his statutes which are written in this book of the law, and if thou turn unto the Lord thy God with all thine heart, and with all thy soul. For this commandment which I command thee this day, it is not hidden from thee, neither is it far off. It is not in heaven, that thou shouldest say, Who shall go up for us to heaven, and bring it unto us, that we may hear it, and do it. Neither is it beyond the sea, that thou shouldest say, Who shall go over the sea for us, and bring it unto us, that we may hear it, and do it. But the word is very nigh unto thee, in thy mouth and in thy heart, that thou mayest do it.

The Holy Spirit is continually at work in our lives when we develop our awareness of the many needs in this world. This level of sensitivity increases as the Holy Spirit takes on a greater purpose in our lives.

Isaiah 11:2 reads, And the spirit of the Lord shall rest upon Him, the Spirit of wisdom and understanding, the Spirit of counsel and might, the Spirit of knowledge and the fear of the Lord.

Feeding of 4,000 men and their families

Jesus is being surrounded by large crowds of people asking Him to heal the lame, the blind, the mute, and many more and they laid them at His feet. Jesus begins to heal them as the crowds grow in numbers and the people begin to realize they are in the presence of their Lord. The crowds continue to grow and people are refusing to leave. In some cases, people have been there for three days without food and shelter. They are afraid if they leave they will miss a blessing.

Mark 8: 1-10 reads, In those days the multitude being very great, and having nothing to eat, Jesus called, his disciples unto him, and saith unto them, "I have compassion on the multitude, because they have now been with me three days, and have nothing to eat. And if I send them away fasting to their own houses, they will faint by the way: for divers of them came from far." And the disciples answered him, From whence can a man satisfy these men with bread here in the wilderness. And he asked them, "How many loaves have ye". And they said seven. And he commanded the people to sit down on the ground: and gave thanks, and brake, and gave to his disciples to set them before the people. And they had a few small fishes: and he blessed, and commanded to set them also before them. So they did eat, and were filled: and they took up of the broken meat that was left seven baskets. So they did eat, and were filled: and they took up of the broken meat that was left seven baskets. And they that had eaten were about four thousand: and he sent them away. And straightway he entered into the ship with his disciples, and came into parts of Delmanutha.

Jesus knew that these people were in need of healing in many ways and He was going to show His mercy to them. The need was great and as in the feeding of the 5,000, food was provided by Jesus as He blessed and broke the bread and used the baskets to distribute this nourishment to his followers. Delmanutha is believed to be located across the sea from Bethsaida on western side of the Sea of Galilee.

As in previous miracles he asked the crowd to be seated and then asked the blessing with the disciples at hand to deliver the bread and fishes. He then gave thanks and He broke the bread and gave it to the disciples for distribution to the crowd. After the feeding of the 4,000 was completed he got into the boat and went to the Magadan area.

Psalm 86: 15 reads, But thou, O Lord, art a God full of compassion, and gracious, long-suffering, and plenteous in mercy and truth.

Psalm 111:4 reads, He hath made his wonderful works to be remembered: the Lord is gracious and full of compassion.

Lamentations 3:22-23 reads, It is of the Lord's mercies that we are not consumed, because his compassions fail not. They are new every morning: great is thy faithfulness.

Jesus' compassion for the people of Israel was limitless. It is imperative that we follow the example set by Jesus and take every opportunity to show compassion to others in our daily lives.

Healing a blind man

The Bible records Jesus healing a number of blind men. In these miracles Jesus places his fingers on the man's eyes with a mixture of saliva and mud.

Mark 8:22-26 reads, And he cometh to Bethsaida: and they bring a blind man unto him and besought him to touch him. And he took the blind man by the hand, and led him out of the town; and when he had spit on his eyes, and put his hands upon him, he asked him if he saw aught. And he looked up, and said, I see men as trees, walking. After that he put his hands again upon his eyes, and made him look up: and he was restored, and saw every man clearly. And He sent him away to his house, saying, "Neither go into the town, nor tell it to any in the town."

Jesus continues to perform miracles and to show His mercy. He leads this man out of town away from the distractions with his disciples. He asked this blind man not to go back to the village and not tell anyone because he knows that the more these miracles are reported the sooner the authorities will come looking to slay him.

Ephesians 3:19-20 reads, And to know the love of Christ, which passeth knowledge, that ye might be filled with all the fullness of God. Now unto him that is able to do exceeding abundantly above all that we ask or think, according to the power that worketh in us.

We need to understand the enormous love God has for us all. He showed his mercy and compassion for this man who was lost and forgotten by society. Jesus was focused on helping the poorest of the poor, those that wandered the cities and villages begging for enough to survived. We need to follow Jesus' example to focus on the poor and their needs.

Psalm 40:17 reads, But I am poor and needy; yet the Lord thinketh upon me: thou art my help and my deliverer; make no tarrying, O my God.

Healing a man born blind

The disciples ask Jesus if this man's blindness was due to sin from his parents or from his sins. Jesus reply was this man's blindness was for the purpose of displaying God's love. God reveals His love and mercy to us in many different ways. We grow in our understanding as we grow in our appreciation of God's love for us.

John 9:1-7 reads, And as Jesus passed by, he saw a man which was blind from his birth. And his disciples asked him, saying Master, who did sin, this man, or his parents, that he was born blind. Jesus answered, "Neither hath this man sinned, nor his parents: but that the works of God should be made manifest in him. I must work the works of him that sent me, while it is day: the night cometh, when no man can work. As long as I am in the world, I am the light of the world." When he has thus spoken, he spat on the ground, and made clay of the spittle, and he anointed the eyes of the blind man with the clay. And he said unto him, "Go, wash in the pool of Siloam". He went his way therefore, and washed, and came seeing.

Again, Jesus performs a miracle knowing that another miracle will cause time to be shortened for His mission. It also needs to be noted, that Jesus explained that His glory is shown in different situations (e.g. this blind man) that are not always easy for us to understand. God's glory and mercy are sometimes worked through blessings that are for our edification. God is teaching us each day as He did with the disciples when He was performing these miracles.

Psalm 69:29-30 reads, But I am poor and sorrowful: let thy salvation, O God, set me up on high. I will praise the name of God, with a song, and will magnify him with thanksgiving.

2 Corinthians 8:9 reads, For ye know the grace of our Lord Jesus Christ, that though he was rich, yet for your sakes he became poor, that ye through his poverty might be rich.

Healing a demon-possessed boy

This miracle is more about faith than it is about casting out demons. Jesus is growing impatient with the disciples and the crowd because of their lack of faith in healing this boy.

Mark 9:17-29 reads, And one of the multitude answered and said, Master, I have brought unto thee my son, which hath a dumb spirit. And wheresoever he taketh him, he teareth him, and he foameth, and gnasheth with his teeth, and pineth away; and I spake to thy disciples that they should cast him out; and they could not. He answered him, and saith, "O faithless generation, how long shall I be with you? how long shall I suffer you? bring him unto me." And they brought him unto him; and when he saw him, straightway the spirit tare him, and he fell on the ground, and wallowed foaming. And he asked his father, "How long is it ago since this came unto him?" And he said, of a child. And ofttimes it hath cast him into the fire, and unto the water, to destroy, but if thou canst do anything, have compassion on us, and help us. Jesus said unto him, "If thou canst believe, all things are possible to him that believeth." And straightway the father of the child cried out, and said with tears, Lord, I believe; help thou mine unbelief. When Jesus saw that the people came running together, he rebuked the foul spirit, saying unto him, "Thou dumb spirit and deaf spirit, I charge thee, come out of him, and enter no more into him." And the spirit cried, and rent him sore, and came out of him: and he was as one dead; insomuch that many said, He is dead. But Jesus took him by the hand, and lifted him up, and he arose.

Again, Jesus is casting out another demon. This demon is preventing this poor boy from speaking normally. This demon was vicious and powerful and capable of tormenting this boy to the point of making him unconscious. The disciples were not able to drive this demon from the boy's body because this was a powerful demon and they did not have enough faith to do so. The amount of faith can be measured by what is accomplished.

Matthew 17:20 reads, And Jesus said unto them, "Because of your unbelief: for verily I say unto you, If ye have faith as a grain of mustard seed, ye shall say unto this mountain, Remove hence to yonder place; and it shall remove: and nothing shall be impossible unto you.

The disciples had at their disposal the power to remove any demon, yet they failed to fully appropriate God's power. Faith comes from not only in the belief in Christ as Savior and Lord, but also in God's revealed Word and will. Faith grows as we study God's word and pray with growing purpose. As we grow in faith we build a reservoir of spiritual power that enables us to be a blessing to others and to accomplish task that would otherwise be impossible.

James 1:3 reads, Knowing this, that the trying of your faith worketh patience. The maturing process requires one to experience difficulties and to be challenged with new issues. Growing in faith requires one to go through difficulties and to experience the power of God as He solves problems through you. The solution to a problem or issue is not always apparent at the time and in some cases it may take years before you understand how His plan was made perfect for your life.

Catching a fish with a coin

This miracle and the payment of the temple tax was for the purpose of revealing both the deity of Jesus and to show to Peter that the Son of God is not obligated to pay tribute for the support of God's house.

Matthew 17: 24-27 reads, And when they were come to Capernaum, they that received tribute money came to Peter, and said, Doth not your master pay tribute? He said, Yes. And when he was come into the house, Jesus prevented him saying, "What thinkest thou, Simon? of whom do the kings of the earth take custom or tribute of their own children, or of strangers?" Peter saith unto him, Of strangers, Jesus said unto him, "Then are the children free? Notwithstanding lest we should offend them, go thou to the sea, and cast a hook, and take up the fish that first cometh up; and when thou hast opened his mouth, thou shalt find a piece of money; that take, and give unto them for me and thee."

Jesus was again teaching the disciples and in this case Peter that Jesus the Son of God was greater than all the temples and should not be subject to any tax. In this miracle, Jesus was showing to Peter his divine power by having a fish provide the tax.

2 Peter 1:3-8 reads, According as his divine power hath given unto us all things that pertain unto life and godliness, through the knowledge of him that hath called us to glory and virtue. Whereby are given unto us exceeding great and precious promises: that by these ye might be partakers of the divine nature, having escaped the corruption that is in the world through lust. And besides this, giving all diligence, add to your faith virtue; and to virtue knowledge. And to knowledge temperance; and to temperance patience; and to patience godliness; And to godliness brotherly kindness; and to brotherly kindness charity. For if these things be in you, and abound, they make you that ye shall neither be barren nor unfruitful in the knowledge of our Lord Jesus Christ.

We are in a lifelong process of maturing in Gods' grace. The one that is able to acquire this degree of maturity with virtue (moral excellence), knowledge (spiritual truth), temperance (self control), patience (endurance), godliness (in his likeness), kindness (brotherly love) and charity (willful love) acquires the rich inheritance in heaven.

Healing a demon possessed man

A demon had possessed this man making him both blind and mute.

Matthew 12: 22-23 reads, Then was brought unto him one possessed with a devil, blind, and dumb: and he healed him, insomuch that the blind and dumb both spake and saw. And all the people were amazed, and said, Is not this the son of David?

Jesus continues to cast out demons and allows these people to regain their lives. Satan is responsible for sin, disease, and death and uses his demons to inflict great pain and suffering.

As other healings this healing also occurred on the Sabbath and resulted in the Pharisees once again objecting to Jesus' act of compassion and accusing Him of working with the devil.

Luke 6:36 reads, "Be ye therefore merciful, as your Father also is merciful."

Psalm 86:15 reads, But thou, O Lord, art a God full of compassion, and gracious, long-suffering, and plenteous in mercy and truth.

Healing a woman with an 18-year infirmity

Luke 13:10-13 reads, And he was teaching in one of the synagogues on the Sabbath. And, behold, there was a woman which had a spirit of infirmity eighteen years, and was bowed together, and could in no wise lift up herself. And Jesus saw her, he called her to him, and said unto her, "Woman thou art loosed from thine infirmity." And he laid his hands on her: and immediately she was made straight, and glorified God.

This woman had a demon spirit that was living within her that was preventing her from standing straight. There are many accounts of people being possessed by demonic powers that are manifested into violent behavior and in some situations crippling a body member.

In this case, it was the Sabbath and Jesus was teaching in the synagogue when he decides to teach about loving your neighbor. He saw a woman possessed by a demon and sets her free from the demon. Jesus is teaching it is more important to free this woman from this demon then it is to follow the law of not working on the Sabbath.

The Sabbath observance was established for the purpose of rest for the body and worship to our Lord and Savior. Jesus pointed out that a farmer would save an ox from a pit on the Sabbath as an act of necessity and mercy. Therefore, showing mercy to a woman and saving her from a demon would certainly be a greater act of necessity and mercy. It is God's message of showing mercy and love to your neighbor that takes on greater importance then the strict rule of absolutely no laboring on the Sabbath. We have Priests that teach God's word in the synagogues and others that prepare food and perform acts of necessity on the Sabbath. They forgot that love is a divine principle and the foundation for the law. Consequently, they intentually used this distortion to charge Jesus with not observing the Sabbath.

Matthew 7:12 reads, "Therefore all things whatsoever ye would that men should do to you, do ye even so to them: for this is the law and the prophets."

Galatians 6:2 reads, Bear ye one another's burdens, and so fulfill the law of Christ.

We are not to stand in judgment of one another, but to show kindness, mercy, patience, forgiveness, and providing comfort to one another.

Healing a man with dropsy

Jesus placed himself in a difficult position by eating and speaking with the lawyers and Pharisees that wished to trap him into breaking the law. The Pharisees were the religious leaders of Israel and many were plotting against Jesus because they saw Jesus as a threat against their rule as religious leaders of the land. However, Jesus took this man with this painful condition and healed him on the Sabbath for all to witness.

Luke 14: 1-6 reads, And it came to pass, as he went into the house of one of the chief Pharisees to eat bread on the Sabbath day, that they watched him. And behold, there was a certain man before him which had the dropsy. And Jesus answering spake unto the lawyers and Pharisees, saying, "Is it lawful to heal on the Sabbath day?" And they held their peace. And he took him, and healed him, and let him go. And answered them, saying, "Which of you shall have an ass or an ox fallen into a pit, and will not straightway pull him out on the Sabbath day?" And they could not answer him again to these things.

Dropsy (Edema) is the building up of fluids in the tissues and the body. Jesus is teaching that Jewish law should recognize that it is important to have mercy on both animals and humans on the Sabbath.

2 Corinthians 3:15 reads, But even unto this day, when Moses is read, the veil is upon their heart. Nevertheless, when it shall turn to the Lord, the veil shall be taken away. Now the Lord is that Spirit: and where the Spirit of the Lord is, there is liberty.

There is a veil over the hearts of the Jews and they are not willing to accept Jesus and the revelation of His message. The Spirit will regenerate the heart and faith will provide the liberty to realize Gods' blessings and rejoice in His love.

Philippians 4:8 reads, Finally, brethren, whatsoever things are true, whatsoever things are honest, whatsoever things are just, whatsoever things are pure, whatsoever things are lovely, whatsoever things are of good report, if there be any virtue, and if there be any praise, think on these things.

The peace of God passes all understanding and may be obtained and sustained by thinking on the right things and working on the right projects. May the God of peace be with you and comfort you throughout your entire life.

Healing of 10 lepers

Jesus was traveling back to Jerusalem along the border of Galilee and Samaria when he was met by 10 lepers along the road. The ten men knew that Jesus was traveling this direction and they waited along the road to beg for mercy.

Luke 17: 11-19 reads, And it came to pass, as he went to Jerusalem, that he passed through the midst of Samaria and Galilee. And as he entered into a certain village, there met him ten men that were lepers, which stood afar off. And they lifted up their voices, and said, Jesus, Master, have mercy on us. And when he saw them, he said unto them, "Go show yourselves unto the priests." And it came to pass, that, as they went, they were cleansed. And one of them, when he saw that he was healed, turned back, and with a loud voice glorified God. And fell down on his face at his feet, giving him thanks: and he was a Samaritan. And Jesus answering said, "Were there not ten cleansed? But where are the nine? There are not found that returned to give glory to God, save the stranger." And he said unto him, "Arise go thy way: thy faith hath made thee whole."

All ten men turned in faith and started to travel to the temple and were immediately healed. However, only the Samaritan (Gentile hated by the Jews) returns to thank God for this blessing and only he receives the complete blessing of salvation. Praising and thanking God for his blessings is a critical element in receiving God's complete blessing.

Phil. 4:6 reads, Be careful for nothing; but in every thing by prayer and supplication with thanksgiving let your requests be made known unto God.

Psalm 26:7 reads, That I may publish with the voice of thanksgiving, and tell of all thy wondrous works.

Colossians 4:2 reads, Continue in prayer, and watch in the same with thanksgiving.

We are to be aware of our surrounding and to be sensitive to the blessings that we receive on a daily basis. Our prayers of thanksgiving act as a seal that we know God is at work in our lives and we are deeply appreciative of His love for us. These prayers need to be presented with the attitude of thanksgiving so that these prayers are preserved with a grateful heart.

God is eager to hear your requests, but they need to be accompanied with an attitude of thanksgiving.

Raising of Lazarus

This miracle is truly remarkable. Raising a man who has been dead for four days is a wonder that only the deity of God could make possible.

John 11:38-44 reads, Jesus therefore again groaning in himself cometh to the grave. It was a cave, and a stone lay upon it. Jesus said, "Take ye away the stone." Martha, the sister of him that was dead, saith unto him, Lord, by this time he stinketh: for he hath been dead four days. Jesus saith unto her, "said I not unto thee, that, if thou wouldest believe, thou shouldest see the glory of God." Then they took away the stone from the place where the dead was laid. And Jesus lifted up his eyes, and said, "Father, I thank thee that thou hast heard me. And I knew that thou hearest me always: but because of the people which stand by I said it, that they may believe that thou hast sent me." And when he thus had spoken, he cried with a loud voice, "Lazarus, come forth." And he that was dead came forth, bound hand and foot with grave clothes: and a napkin. Jesus saith unto them, "Loose him, and he let him go."

When Jesus saw Mary and the Jews weeping for Lazarus, he also groaned in spirit and wept for the sorrow sin had brought into the world with sickness and death. John recognized the full humanity of Jesus as well as his deity. Martha tried to intercede by recognizing that the body of Lazarus had began to decompose, however, Jesus reminder Martha of God's glory and the power of the Father of all creation. At this point, Jesus raised his eyes to heaven and called upon his Father to break the hold death had on Lazarus with a prayer of thanksgiving for the constant communion bond of understanding and grace.

Isaiah 25:8 reads, He will swallow up death in victory; and the Lord God, will wipe away tears from off faces; and the rebuke of his people shall be take away from off all the earth: for the Lord hath spoken it.

1 Corinthians 15:54-55 reads, So when this corruptible shall have put on incorruption, and this mortal shall have put on immortality, then shall be brought to pass the saying that is written, Death is swallowed up in victory. O Death, Where is thy Sting? O Grave, where is thy Victory?

Those that have died in Christ shall be raised as incorruptible. Death may be the result of sin and the triumph of Satan. However, it was the death of God's Son and his resurrection that defeated death and redeemed us all from a life of darkness.

Healing of Bartimaeus of blindness

Jesus was traveling to Jericho when he came upon Bartimaeus a blind man that was begging along the road. Bartimaeus heard that Jesus was near and he started calling "Jesus, Son of David". There was a large crowd of people and great deal of noise, but Jesus heard his call and asked that he come forward.

Mark 10: 46-52 reads, And they came to Jericho: and as he went out of Jericho with his disciples and a great number of people, blind Bartimeus, the son of Timaeus, sat by the highway side begging. And when he heard that it was Jesus of Nazareth, he began to cry out, and say, Jesus, thou son of David, have mercy on me. And many charged him that he should hold his peace: but he cried the more a great deal. Thou son of David, have mercy on me. And Jesus stood still, and commanded him to be called. And they call the blind man, saying unto him, Be of good comfort, rise; he calleth thee. And he, casting away his garment, rose, and came to Jesus. And Jesus answered and said unto him, "What wilt thou that I should do unto thee?" The blind man said unto him, Lord, that I might receive my sight. And Jesus said unto him, "Go thy way; thy faith hath made thee whole." And immediately he received his sight, and followed Jesus in the way.

This blind beggar got the attention of Jesus by calling him the Son of David, thereby recognizing Jesus as the promised Messiah.

This healing was the direct result of this man's faith, his persistence, and his eagerness. Jesus again showed his compassion and love for his neighbors and again revealed to his disciples the importance of recognizing those in need and to provide assistance.

Romans 4:20 reads, He staggered not at the promise of God through unbelief; but was strong in faith, giving glory to God.

Proverbs 28:20 reads, A faithful man shall abound with blessings: but he that maketh haste to be rich shall not be innocent.

As can be read in the Septuagint (Proverbs 20:6-8), A man is valuable; and a merciful man precious: but it is hard to find a faithful man. He that walks blameless in justice, shall leave his children blessed.

Withering of the fig tree

This miracle is a simple parable that shows that our life needs to be fruitful and to be actively involved in furthering God's kingdom.

The more we understand God and his purpose the more creditable these miracles become and the more we grow in appreciation. We have this formless life power within us that allows us to tap into the infinite power of God himself. From God flows beauty, truth, goodness, and a spiritual force that allows miracles to be completed in our daily lives. These miracles occur in perfect harmony with all that exists and allows all to become an active member in a life changing event. It is your prayers through faith that allow these miracles to be completed and for you to complete your purpose.

Mark 11:12-14, 20-25 reads, And on the morrow, when they were come from Bethany, he was hungry. And seeing a fig tree afar off having leaves, he came, if haply he might find any thing thereon: and when he came to it, he found nothing but leaves; for the time of figs was not yet. And Jesus answered and said unto it, "No man eat fruit of thee hereafter for ever." And his disciples heard it. And in the morning, as they passed by, they saw the fig tree dried up from the roots. And Peter calling to remembrance saith unto him, Master behold, the fig tree which thou cursedst is withered away.

And Jesus answering said unto them. "Have faith in God." "For verily I say unto you, That whosoever shall say unto this mountain, Be thou removed, and be thou cast into sea; and shall not doubt in his heart, but shall believe that those things which he saith shall come to pass; he shall have whatsoever he saith." "Therefore I say unto you, What things soever ye desire, when ye pray, believe that ye receive them and ye shall have them." "And when ye stand praying forgive, if ye have aught against any, that your father also which is in heaven may forgive you your trespasses."

We cannot be like the despised fig tree that appears to be providing fruit, but when tested provides no nourishment. The consequences of not providing fruit could be severe as in the case of this fig tree. Jesus reminds his disciples to have faith in God and to ask, "and shall not doubt in his heart, but shall believe that those things which he saith shall come to pass; he shall have whatsoever he saith." We are to pray in complete confidence that all issues will be resolved within God's almighty providence. Your faith needs to be without question and completely submerged and in complete harmony with God's eternal love. This Eternal love allows us to live this life that is but a whisper in time. We need to be conscious of this shortness in time and to be vigilant to ensure our lives are under God's direction and to be open to His will. The passage also reminds the disciples that they need to be on guard not to break their relationship with God with an unforgiving spirit. We need to be on guard not to allow Satan to influence our lives and develop an unforgiving spirit within us. This can be a daily battle that requires time with prayer and scripture study.

Jeremiah 24: 3-7 reads, Then said the Lord unto me, What seest thou, Jeremiah? And I said, Figs; the good figs, very good; and the evil, very evil, that cannot be eaten, they are so evil. Again the word of the Lord came unto me, saying. Thus saith the Lord, the God of Israel; Like these good figs, so will I acknowledge them that are carried away captive of Judah, whom I have sent out of this place into the land of the Chaldeans for their good. For I will set mine eyes upon them for good, and I will bring them again to this land: and I will build them, and not pull them down; and I will plant them, and not pluck them up. And I will give them a heart to know me, that I am the Lord; and they shall be my people, and I will be their God: for they shall return to me with their whole heart.

Jeremiah is saying the unfruitful fig tree symbolizes Israel's refusal to respond to God's word and that evil is like rotten figs that cannot be eaten. God gives us time to get right with him, but that time is now. A death can be sudden and without warning and can leave one without time to repent of one's sins. If we delay we may find grace has passed us.

Miracle of healing a severed ear

At the Mount of Olives, Jesus and his disciples are confronted by soldiers in an effort to arrest him and take him captive. Judas Iscariot had betrayed him and told the authorities of his location. During this confrontation, one of the Jesus' followers severed the ear of one of the servants of the chief priest. Jesus healed this man's ear and allowed himself to be arrested.

Luke 22:47-51 reads, And while he yet spake, behold a multitude, and he that was called Judas, one of the twelve, went before them, and drew near unto Jesus to kiss him. But Jesus said unto him, "Judas betrayest thou the Son of man with a kiss." When they which were about him saw what would follow, they said unto him, Lord, shall we smite with the sword? And one of them smote the servant of the high priest, and cut off his right ear. And Jesus answered and said, "Suffer ye thus far". And he touched his right ear, and healed him.

John 18:10 reads, Then Simon Peter having a sword drew it, and smote the high priest's servant, and cut off his right ear. The servant's name was Malchus.

Only John gives the name of the disciple that cut off the servant's ear and only John gives us the name of the servant, Malchus. John was one of the three inner disciples and was often found with Peter and James. All three disciples were in the Garden of Gethsemane at the foot of the Mount of Olives with Jesus when He was betrayed by Judas.

These men came in darkness so that their identity may not be known to the multitude of believers. Jesus acknowledges that Satan comes in the darkness and is near and is working among these men.

Ephesians 6:12 reads, For we wrestle not against flesh and blood, but against principalities, against powers, against the ruler of the darkness of this world, against spiritual wickedness in high places.

We are in a spiritual battle with different ranks of demons that are hosts of Satan that are the rulers of the world's darkness. We need to hold fast to our salvation, righteousness, truth, faith, and God's Holy Spirit. We need to stand firm and hold our position with the Lord Jesus Christ himself.

I Thessalonians 5:17-24 reads, Pray without ceasing. In everything give thanks: for this is the will of God in Christ Jesus concerning you. Quench not the Spirit. Despise not prophesying. Prove all things; hold fast that which is good. Abstain from all appearance of evil. And the very God of peace sanctify you wholly; and I pray God your whole spirit and soul and body be preserved blameless unto the coming of our Lord Jesus Christ. Faithful is he that calleth you, who also will do it.

The resurrection of Jesus Christ

The empty tomb was the first undeniable fact that Jesus was no longer here on the earth. The Roman government and the Jewish authorities were aware of the resurrection prophecies and to ensure no one removed the body from the tomb it was sealed with a huge rock and guarded by soldiers throughout the night.

The resurrection was a complete surprise to the disciples and to the women who traveled to the tomb with oils, spices, and burial materials to prepare the body of Jesus. When the women approached the tomb they found that the stone had been rolled away and when they entered they could not find the body of Jesus.

Mark 16: 5-7 reads, And entering into the sepulcher, they saw a young man sitting on the right side, clothed in a long white garment: and they were affrighted. And he saith unto them, Be not affrighted: Ye seek Jesus of Nazareth, which was crucified: he is risen; he is not here: behold the place where they laid him. But go your way, tell his disciples and Peter that he goeth before you into Galilee: there shall ye see him, as he said unto you.

Even though Jesus had spoken of his death and resurrection on the third day, the disciples did not completely understand what would transpire. The crucifixion was without a doubt an experience that exhausted and demoralized the disciples and all the followers. In some cases they hid for fear they would be next.

John 18: 26-27 reads, When Jesus therefore saw his mother, and the disciple standing by, whom he loved, he saith unto his mother, "Woman behold thy son". Then saith he to the disciple, "Behold thy mother" And from that hour that disciple took her unto his own home.

At that time when Jesus said, "It is finished" the disciples disbursed in fear and continued to grieve. They did not go to the grave site the next morning, until Mary Magdalene ran to Peter and told him all that she had seen.

John 20:2-5 reads, Then she runneth, and cometh to Simon Peter, and to other disciples, whom Jesus loved, and saith unto them. They have taken away the Lord out of the sepulcher, and we know not where they have laid him. Peter therefore went forth, and that other disciple, and came to the sepulcher. So they ran both together: and the other disciples did outrun Peter, and came first to the sepulcher. And he stooping down, and looking in, saw the linen clothes lying: yet went he not in. Then cometh Simon Peter following him, and went into the sepulcher, and seeth the linen clothes lie. And the napkin, that was about his head, not lying with the linen clothes, but wrapped together in a place by itself. Then went in also that other disciple, which came first to the sepulcher, and he saw, and believed.

Simon Peter and the disciples ran in a panic to the sepulcher not knowing what had happen to the body of Jesus. What was going through their minds? Did someone steal the body? They knew the tomb was guarded by soldiers. They did not remember or consider what Jesus had told them that He would be raised on the third day. It was Mary Magdalene that remained at the sepulcher weeping not knowing what to think.

John 20:11-18 reads, But Mary stood without at the sepulcher weeping: and as she wept, she stooped down, and looked into the sepulcher. And seeth two angels in white sitting, the one at the head, and the other at the feet, where the body of Jesus had lain. And they say unto her, Woman, why weepest thou? She saith unto them, Because they have taken away my Lord, and I know not where they have laid him. And when she had thus said, she turned herself back, and saw Jesus standing, and knew not that it was Jesus. Jesus saith unto her, 'Woman, why weepest thou? Whom seekest thou?" She supposing him to be the gardener saith unto him, Sir, if thou have borne him hense, tell me where thou hast laid him, and I will take him away. Jesus saith unto her, "Mary", she turned herself, and saith unto him, Rabboni; which is to say, Master. Jesus saith unto her, "Touch me not; for I am not yet ascended to my Father: but go my brethren, and say unto them, I ascend unto my Father, and your Father; and to my God, and your God." Mary Magdalene came and told the disciples that she had seen the Lord, and that he had spoken these things unto her.

The disciples, family, friends, and Mary Magdalene were overcome in grief and experiencing extreme sorrow and were in a panic over the death of Jesus and now the disappearance of His body. Mary Magdalene alone next to the sepulcher, sees the two angels within the tomb and they ask, "Why weepest thou". She still does not understand that her Lord has defeated death and was still with her. It isn't until Jesus himself addresses her as Mary that she realize that Jesus was alive and there with her. The disciples had gone from days in the depths of grieving to a place of disbelief.

Mary Magdalene, Joanna, and Mary the mother of James are the first to grasp and believe that Jesus has risen and are enthusiastically explaining to the disciples what the angels had told Mary Magdalene. Mary Magdalene had gained a position of prominence among the disciples, but had come from a past of immorality. Jesus had also healed her of mental and physical infirmities.

Luke 8:2 reads, And certain women, which had been healed of evil spirits and infirmities, Mary called Magdalene, out of whom went seven devils.

Jesus again teaches his disciples that he uses individuals that they may not consider to be the best candidate for a position. Why? They need to realize that God knows each person's soul and Spirit and He alone will determine the best vessel for the His message. As we grow in faith we are able to discern and recognize His message and direction.

Jesus then appears to the disciples and allows them to see his hands and his side. Then the disciples believed and were satisfied and took joy in the realization of the resurrection of their Lord and Savior.

1 Corinthians 15:17 reads, And if Christ be not raised, your faith is vain: ye are yet in your sins.

William Tyndale wrote, "The Law and Gospel are two keys. The law is the key that shutteth up all men under condemnation, and the gospel is the key which opens the door and lets them out."

The Law acts as a sentinel protecting us, guarding us and directing us to a path of righteousness and allowing us to accept the gift of salvation through faith. The law is meant to prepare man for Jesus Christ, by showing them that there is no other way of salvation except by believing in Him and turning control over to Him. The law impacted man in two ways, it made man realize the deadly effect sin has on man and that there is no escape except through faith in Jesus Christ, and the law prepared a path for the gospel of Christ and a path for salvation for the entire human race.

The miracle of catching fish after the resurrection

Jesus was standing on the shores of Galilee near Capernaum in the early morning when flog and darkness was still hanging over the sea. Jesus calls out to the fishermen in a boat not far from shore.

John 21:4-11 reads, But when the morning was now come, Jesus stood on the shore: but the Disciples knew not that it was Jesus. Then Jesus saith unto them, "Children, have ye any meat?" They answered him, No. And he said unto them, "Cast the net on the right side of the ship, and ye shall find". They cast therefore, and now they were not able to draw it for the multitude of fishes. Therefore that disciple whom Jesus loved saith unto Peter, It is the Lord. Now when Simon Peter heard that it was the Lord, he girt his fisher's coat unto him, (for he was naked,) and did cast himself into the sea. And the other disciples came in a little ship; (for they were not far from land, but as it were two hundred cubits,) dragging the net with fishes. As soon then as they were come to land, they saw a fire of coals there, and fish laid thereon, and bread. Jesus saith unto them, "Bring of the fish which ye have now caught". Simon Peter went up, and drew the net to land full of great fishes, a hundred and fifty and three: and for all there were so many, yet was not the net broken.

Jesus after His crucifixion and resurrection is standing triumphal on the shore in His in deity and in a body that allows the disciples to see him and touch him. He shows himself in a spiritual body that was raised, but also in a glorified body, that the disciples are able to see and hear His words and direction. The disciples did not recognize Jesus in the early morning light when he called to them asking if they caught any fish. They followed the stranger's directions and soon realized that it was their Lord standing on the shore when their nets were filled with fish.

At this time Jesus meets with seven of the disciples on the shores of Galilee for a breakfast of fish and bread. He spends time with them as we should spend time with one another in sharing our concerns and prayer requests. We may spend many hours striving as these disciples and have little success, until we are open (i.e., humble, contrite spirit) to the suggestions of others that are in the divine providence of God's word and cast our nets on the other side of the boat. We need to remember our Lord is compassionate and is waiting for us to submit our requests to Him on a daily basis.

Our prayers must be submitted with a cleansed heart that has confessed all sin.

Psalm 66:18 reads, If I regard iniquity in my heart, the Lord will not hear me.

We must approach God in prayer as a sinner acknowledging we all are in need of salvation. We are to acknowledge our sin, turn from it, and accept the grace of God.

1 John 1:9 reads, If we confess our sins, he is faithful and just to forgive us our sins, and to cleanse us from all unrighteousness.

We need to recognize our daily sins that may come from many different sources (e.g., attitudes), and recognize them for what they are and ask for forgiveness. Our prayers also need to be presented in faith.

James 1: 5-8 reads, If any of you lack wisdom, let him ask of God, that giveth to all men liberally, and upbraideth not; and it shall be given him. But let him ask in faith, nothing wavering. For he that wavereth is like a wave of the sea driven with wind and tossed. For let not that man think that he shall receive any thing of the Lord. A double-minded man is unstable in all his ways.

God is unchanging because He is perfect in every way. Without faith it is impossible to please God. Our prayers are submitted in the faith of Christ.

The ascension of Jesus

Forty days had passed since the crucifixion and resurrection of Jesus. During this time Jesus has spent time with his disciples in training them and sharing with them the reality of his resurrection.

Acts 1: 1-11 reads, The former treatise have I made. O Theophilus, of all that Jesus began both to do and teach. Until the day in which he was taken up, after that he through the Holy Ghost had given commandments unto the apostles whom he had chosen: To whom also he showed himself alive after his passion be many infallible proofs, being seen of them forty days, and speaking of things pertaining to the kingdom of God. And being assembled together with them, commanded them that they should not depart from Jerusalem, but wait for the promise of the father, "which", saith he,"ye have heard of me". "For John truly baptized with water, but ye shall be baptized with the Holy Ghost not many days hense." When they therefore were come together, they asked of him, saying, Lord, wilt thou at this time restore again the kingdom to Israel? And he said unto them, "It is not for you to know the times or the season, which the Father hath put in his own power." "But ye shall receive power, after that the Holy Ghost is come upon you: and ye shall be witnesses unto me both in Jerusalem, and in all Judea, and in Samaria, and unto the uttermost part of the earth." And when he had spoken these things, while they beheld, he was taken up; and a cloud received him out of their sight. And while they looked steadfastly toward heaven as he went up, behold, two men stood by them in white apparel. Which also said, Ye men of Galilee, why stand ye gazing up into the heaven? This same Jesus, which is taken up from you into heaven, shall so come in like manner as ye have seen him go into heaven.

On the Mount of Olives (a Sabbath day's journey from Jerusalem) the disciples watched as Jesus ascended into heaven. At this time angels appeared for the purpose of explaining to the disciples that Jesus has ascended and would no longer be visible to them. The angels also explain that He would return one day in the same glorious way.

This was the final appearance of Jesus on earth until the second coming when he will be visible to all mankind.

Zechariah 14:4 reads, And his feet shall stand in that day upon the mount of Olives, which is before Jerusalem on the east, and the mount of Olives shall cleave in the midst thereof toward the east and toward the west, and there shall be a very great valley; and half of the mountain shall remove toward the north, and half of it toward the south.

The prophet Zechariah (estimate 520 B.C.) foretells the centuries of hatred of Israel and its destruction with many nations dividing the spoils. It is in this darkest of hours when the second coming will happen and God will appear in the sky for all to see Him and to return to the same place (Mount of Olives) where He ascended many years before with His disciples watching in wonder.

At this time there will be a glorious appearance of the Son of God, the Lord God himself with all of the saints, and all of the angels.

Satan and his Demons

SATAN AND HIS FOLLOWERS have had a long history of trying to destroy God's kingdom, the gift of salvation through Jesus Christ and his ministry. After the fall of man, Satan was given authority over death, disease, and sin. It was only when Jesus died on the cross and arose from the grave that the head of Satan was crushed and his powers were further limited. At this point Satan was rendered powerless over spiritual death. It is only those individuals and their spirits that have made a decision to believe in Jesus that will survive the final judgment.

Hebrews 2:14-15 reads, Foreasmuch then as the children are partakers of the flesh and blood, he also himself likewise took part of the same; that through death he might destroy him that had the power of death, that is the devil; And delivered them who through fear of death were all their lifetime subject to bondage.

Those individuals who have spirits that have been aligned with Satan will be dead to God. They are individuals who's spirits have lived in the lust of the flesh and have been working with those of disobedience.

Genesis 3:14-15 reads, And I will put enmity between thee and the women, and between thy seed and her seed; it shall bruise thy head, and thou shalt bruise his heel.

The entire earth was affected by the fall and Satan was cursed for eternity. Adam did not remember the positive effect of obedience and the disastrous results of disobedience.

1 John 3:8 reads, He that committed sin is of the devil; for the devil sinneth from the beginning. For this purpose the Son of God was manifested, that he might destroy the works of the devil.

When Jesus died on the cross and arose from the grave three days later He defeated death and destroyed Satan's power over spiritual death. God's greatest of sacrifices (the Son of God) sealed those that have made the decision to believe in God and obey his commandments. They would have no need to fear spiritual death because their sins have been forgiven. It is only those who believe that are under the protection of God Almighty.

Satan is a roaring lion that is continually roaming, looking to devour another soul. Satan and his demons have great power and can only harm a believer if they allow their faith and obedience to be compromised. Consequently, we need to resist the devil and his demons on a daily basis by praying to our Lord to lead us from temptation and to deliver us from evil.

1 Peter 5:8 reads, Be sober, be vigilant; because your adversary the devil, as a roaring lion, walketh about, seeking whom he may devour.

Matthew 6:13 reads, "And lead us not into temptation but deliver us from evil: For thine is the kingdom, and the power, and the glory, for ever Amen.

The true living almighty God has provided His blessing for all of mankind and continues to reveal His divine character in answering the prayers of the faithful. Jesus was the instrument that God used to reveal His almighty power through miracles that illustrated his divine authority over all His creation.

Miracles Today

There is some controversy within our society and the church about miracles that are occurring today. Part of the issue is that we have a fallen nature that involves pride, greed, lust and other sins that impede man from seeing God's miracles. Other related sins are based on unconfessed sin, resentments or deep seated psychosomatic conflicts that have not been resolved that are preventing an open communion with the Holy Spirit. We are both a physical and spiritual being that results in both our physical capacity and spirits taking part in what we perceive and the decisions and actions we take throughout each day. However, our society is filled with many people that do not believe in God or have no interest in anything related to the church and therefore, do not believe in miracles or anything they do not see or cannot be proven by science. As from the beginning of time many people have refused to believe in miracles, even those that have been physically present when miracles have occurred. Even some of the disciples did not believe in the miracle of Jesus' resurrection until Jesus showed them his pierced hands. Unfortunately, mans' fallen nature and his refusal to address his sins will prevent many from receiving God's blessings.

The cross and the resurrection changed the entire world in many different ways. We only understand a small part of God's love, wisdom and need to be in continual contact asking for insight as to His plans and direction. Consequently, we do not understand all the ramifications related to the cross and the resurrection and how His love has affected each one of us.

Romans 16:20 reads, And the God of peace shall bruise Satan under your feet shortly. The grace of our Lord Jesus Christ be with you. Amen.

The cross and the resurrection crushed Satan further limiting his power and causing him to work in the dark shadows. He continues with his perversion of men's minds with the ultimate goal for the complete destruction of society. Satan's influences are intended to encourage self-centeredness, greed, pride, and to separate us from God's love.

The cross and the resurrection resulted in the Holy Spirit taking on a more active role in the daily lives of Christians.

1 Corinthians 6:11 reads, And such were some of you: but ye are washed, but ye are sanctified, but ye are justified in the name of the Lord Jesus, and by the Spirit of our Lord.

The Spirit of God dwells within the Christian's daily life by providing direction and providing strength where we are weak. The road to sanctification is a long road that requires us to struggle with the building of the faith, for patience to endurance, and to the love of God. Paul's prayer is that we all would be able to stand perfect and complete in the word of God.

Colossians 4:12 reads, Epaphras, who is one of you, a servant of Christ, saluteth you, always laboring fervently for you in prayers, that ye may stand perfect and complete in all the will of God.

We sin each day in many different ways. However, when that day comes when we are ushered into God's presence we pray we will have reached that point in our lives where maturity and assurance has preceded us.

The Holy Spirits also intercedes for us in communicating to God in ways we are not able to. He presents our prayers in way so that God hears them.

Romans 8:26 reads, Likewise the Spirit also helpeth our infirmities: for we know not what we should pray for as we ought: but the Spirit itself maketh intercession for us with groaning which cannot be uttered.

The Holy Spirit intercedes for us by presenting our prayers and pledging for His mercy that our lives may be in His will.

The death and the resurrection also changed where and how the disciples worshiped. The disciples were initially always in the temple asking for God's direction, forgiveness, and blessings. They began to break bread in each other's homes and continued teaching and preaching about Jesus outside the temple. There was no longer any need to make sacrifices for the forgiveness of sins at the temple since Jesus paid it all with His sacrifice at the cross.

The time for worship changed as Christians began to gather not on the Sabbath, but on Sunday the day in which Jesus Christ arose from the grave and defeated death.

The cross, the resurrection, and the Holy Spirit inspired the scriptures and allowed man to read the scriptures and to receive truth. We need to read the scriptures with an open heart and apply these truths to our daily lives. God's eternal plan was to be crucified as a result of man's rebellious act due to the access of free will. We too are therefore responsible for this action.

The Protestant Reformation brought about a renewed approach to scripture as God's authoritative and inspired word. It was Martin Luther that stood up against the Catholic Church and made the point that his teachings were based on the true word on God.

2 Samuel 23:2-5 reads, The Spirit of the Lord spake by me, and his word was in my tongue. The God of Israel said, the Rock of Israel spake to me, he that ruleth over men must be just, ruling in the fear of God. And he shall be as the light of the morning, when the sun riseth, even a morning without clouds; as the tender grass springing out of the earth by clear shining after rain. Although my house be not so with God; yet he hath made with me an everlasting covenant, ordered in all things, and sure: for this is all my salvation, and all my desire, although he make it not to grow.

David is professing that his inspiration was from the Holy Spirit and that he has an unconditional covenant with his Lord. Although David was a sinner, God spoke through David. God is ever faithful and blessed Israel regardless of her failures.

John 16: 5-11 reads, "But now go my way to him that sent me; and none of you asketh me, Whither goest thou? But because I have said these things unto you, sorrow hath filled your heart.

Nevertheless I tell you the truth; It is expedient for you that I go away: for if I go not away, the Comforter will not come unto you; but if I depart, I will send him unto you. And when he is come, he will reprove the world of sin, and of righteousness, and of judgment. Of sin, because they believe not on me. Of righteousness, because I go to my Father, and ye see me no more; Of judgment, because the prince of this world is judged."

Jesus explained to the disciples that He would leave them, but at the same time He would always be with them through the Holy Ghost.

We need to realize that the Holy Ghost is present in our daily lives and that we need to allow him to take control of our thoughts, words, actions, and emotions. It is the Holy Ghost that sanctifies our lives to the point where we are presentable to our Lord. He convicts us of our sins by making us realize that we to move ahead in His plan. The Holy Ghost is continually present in our daily lives and ensures us that God loves us, that God has a plan for us, and that we are completely dependent on God for his mercy and grace. We are dependent on the Holy Ghost to direct us from the sin we encounter each day and to show us the way to truth and love for our neighbor. The Holy Ghost communes with our spirits to strengthen our faith and to recognize the righteousness of Christ our Savior. The Holy Ghost will be with us as we stand before God's judgment.

William Tyndale wrote the following:

But right faith is a thing wrought by the Holy Ghost in us, turneth us into a new nature, and begetteh us anew in God, and maketh us the sons of God, as thee readeth in the first of John: and killeth the old Adam, and maketh us altogether new in the heart, mind, will, lust, and in affections and powers of the soul; the Holy Ghost ever accompanying her, and ruling the heart.

When the scriptures are read or heard the Spirit of God enters into the heart and makes us realize the importance of obedience, the sin that exists in our lives, and the importance of asking for forgiveness. The Holy Ghost communes with our soul and heals us of our nature as we grow in love of our Savior's mercy.

Jesus completed many miracles and healed many people of many different infirmities, but many people still did not believe He was their Lord and Savior. For many to admit they believed in Jesus would be disastrous for them in many ways. It would mean they would be expelled from the temple and criticized by the religious leaders and maybe in some cases may be placed in danger. They would have to face the fact that their beliefs and their way of life needed to change. Jesus realized that many people would not believe even after witnessing miracles.

Luke 16:31 reads, "And he said unto him, If they hear not Moses and the prophets, neither will they be persuaded, though one rose from the dead."

Jesus was saying that miracles by themselves do not produce faith. Even after Jesus rose from the dead people still did not believe He was their Lord and Savior. It is only at that point in time when they surrender and believe in Jesus the Christ that the Holy Spirit enters into their being and communes with their soul that they are saved for eternity. At this point the greatest of all miracles occurs and that is when a person's soul is given eternal life.

Jesus completed many miracles and signs in the presence of the disciples that are not recorded in the scriptures so that the disciples may believe. However, Jesus completed many miracles that are recorded in the scriptures for the purpose that we may believe in the Son of God and follow his direction each day.

John 20:30-31 reads, And many other signs truly did Jesus in the presence of his disciples, which are not written in this book. But these are written, that ye might believe that Jesus is the Christ, the Son of God; and that believing ye might have life through His name.

The Apostle John wrote these words for our knowledge in knowing that these recorded miracles are for our edification of faith in Jesus Christ and an encouragement and that nothing is impossible with God. God who created the world and the universe has all authority, all power, all wisdom, and is continually revealing His love for those souls waiting for His return.

Lamentations 3:25 reads, The Lord is good unto them that wait for him, to the soul that seeketh him.

Martin Luther wrote,

"And though this world with devils filled,
Should threaten to undo us,
we will not fear,
for God hath willed His truth to triumph through us."

There is no question that God has sovereign power over the entire universe and those that dwell within.

The day of Pentecost was the annual feast that fell on the seventh Sunday following the day of the first fruits. The disciples were all gathered together at this time in Jerusalem when they were all filled by the Holy Spirit. The Holy Spirit came as a violent wind and a fire that rested on each person present. The filling of the Holy Spirit may occur a number of times after a person has made a confession of faith and is baptized.

Acts 2: 1-7 reads, And when the day of Pentecost was fully come, they were all with one accord in one place. And suddenly there came a sound from heaven as of a rushing mighty wind, and it filled all the house where they were sitting. And there appeared unto them cloven tongues like as of fire, and it sat upon each of them. And they were all filled with the Holy Ghost, and began to speak with other tongues, as the Spirit gave them utterance. And there were dwelling at Jerusalem Jews, devout men, out of every nation under heaven. Now when this was noised abroad, the multitude came together, and were confounded, because that every man heard them speak in his own language. And they were all amazed and marveled, saying one to another, Behold, are not all these which speak Galileans?

We are in prayer each day thanking Him for His many blessing and asking for the direction of the Holy Ghost. We do not always see God's hand in our daily lives, but as we survey the past we are amazed and overwhelmed how He has guided us every step as we travel through life's journey. I have experienced a life time of blessings that were folded out in His Word, the Spirit, and the situations that were arranged in His glorious plan. When our Lord came to earth and took on the limitations and temptations of humanity, he was under the complete submission of God's will.

John 14:10 reads, "Believest thou not that I am in the Father, and the Father in me? The words that I speak unto you I speak not of myself: but the Father that dwelleth in me, he doeth the works."

His example to us is that we must be in complete submission to God's word to be within His plan for us.

Romans 8:38-39 reads, For I am persuaded, that neither death, nor life, nor angels, nor principalities, nor powers, nor things present, nor things to come, nor height, nor depth, nor any other creature, shall be able to separate us from the love of God, which is in Christ Jesus our Lord.

God loves us and wants to show his glory to us throughout every day. He is our father and wants to give us all good things.

Ephesians 5:15-18 reads, See then that ye walk circumspectly, not as fools, but as wise, redeeming the time, because the days are evil. Wherefore be ye not unwise, but understanding what the will of the Lord is. And be not drunk with wine, wherein is excess; but be filled with the Spirit.

We need to be careful how we live and that we live our lives in God's plan and will. We need to be aware of our surroundings and to be sensitive to the direction of the Holy Spirit. There is a close relationship that is developed between the Christian and Holy Spirit. As this relationship grows and becomes stronger the Christian becomes more aware and dependent on the Holy Spirit. The Christian learns that there are many aspects to this relationship and that it takes time to understand how circumstances and opportunities come together for His perfect plan for our life. A filling process occurs as the Holy Spirit takes on a greater role in a Christian life. If allowed this filling process will continue throughout a Christian's life.

God's word and His scriptures are the primary avenues for the Holy Spirit to communicate with believers.

2 Timothy 3:16 reads, All scripture is given by inspiration of God, and is profitable for doctrine, for reproof, for correction, for instruction in righteousness: that the man of God may be perfect, thoroughly furnished unto all good works.

The scriptures were written for the purpose of growth and the maturity of man. These scriptures are used by the Holy Spirit to convict man of his sin and to allow him to change his ways. The scriptures are also used as a method for training and allowing man to grow to righteousness. Paul in these verses is reminding Timothy that all scripture is God-breathed and will be useful in all aspect of his ministry. Paul was confident in Timothy and knows he was committed and knows that God will provide for all his needs through the scriptures. For the Holy Spirit to take on a more active role in our lives we need to be in study of his word each day and allow our souls to hear his voice and direction. The Holy Spirit is with us throughout the day and will bring into our life situations and people that will provide opportunities and direction.

John 14: 16-17 reads, "And I will pray the Father, and he shall give you another Comforter, that he may abide with you for ever; Even the Spirit of truth; whom the world cannot receive, because it seeth him not, neither knoweth him, but ye know him, for he dwelleth with you, and shall be in you."

God provides the Holy Spirit to his believers knowing that many will experience persecution from many different sources and in many different ways. The Holy Spirit comes to the believer as a presence that dwells within a person that cannot be seen or heard by the world. Society and the world are governed and restricted by the human senses of sight, hearing, feelings, and taste. Therefore, there is no method for the world to recognize the existence of the Holy Spirit, the works of the Holy Spirit, and the miracles that occur on a daily basis.

John 16:13 reads, Howbeit when he, the Spirit of truth, is come, he will guide you into all truth: for he shall not speak of himself; but whatsoever he shall hear, that shall he speak: and he will show you things to come.

As believers we not only recognize the Holy Spirit, we are engaged in rejoicing with the Holy Spirit in fellowship. As this relationship develops with the Holy Spirit we quickly realize the limitations of the vessel we live in. Our spirit wants to be free to worship with its Creator. At times the Holy Spirit not only convicts us of our sins but guides us to what is true and the need to prepare ourselves to be able to stand in front of our Savior.

We are looking and listening for miracles and need to acknowledge them when they occur. Each day the Holy Ghost speaks to us through the Bible and provides for us opportunities that we need to take advantage of. We see and hear of signs of His return each day through many different avenues. We are part of His kingdom and in some sense preparing for His return.

God calls us to be holy and to live a life that is separated from sin and evil. To accomplish this we need to live a life that is controlled by the Holy Spirit.

1 Peter 1:16 reads, Because it is written, Be ye Holy; for I am Holy.

Leviticus 19:2 reads, Speak unto all the congregation of the children of Israel, and say unto them, Ye shall be holy: for I the Lord your God am Holy.

Ephesians 1: 13 reads, In whom ye also trusted, after that ye heard, the word of truth, the gospel of your salvation in whom also after that ye believed, ye were sealed with that Holy Spirit of promise.

The Holy Spirit seals your salvation with the promise of eternal life. We need to praise and thank God for this promise and realize the importance of this relationship and be careful not to block and hinder our relationship with the Holy Spirit.

The basic principle of maintaining this relationship with the Holy Spirit is to be obedient to God's word. This is a command that needs to be followed and to be obedient throughout our entire life.

Matthew 5:16 reads, Jesus said, "Let your light so shine before men, that they may see your good works, and glorify your father which is heaven."

Romans 6:6 reads, Knowing this, that our old man is crucified with him, that the Body of sin might be destroyed, that henceforth we should not serve sin.

The purpose of our lives is to glorify God and to thank him for the freedom he gave us from the bondage of sin. The past history of man's sin was destroyed and washed clean by the crucifixion of Jesus on the cross.

1 John 3:24 reads, And he that keepeth his commandments dwelleth in him, and he in him. And hereby we know that he abideth in us, by the Spirit which he hath given us.

The Holy Spirit bears witness that Christ abides in us. The Holy Spirit works within our lives and transforms us to a person that is spiritual. The degree of spirituality is dependent on us and our relationship with our Lord.

Placing God first in your life will require us to grow in appreciation of his creation and to see things as he would see them. To enjoy His creation requires us to have a change in mind set and vision and to grow in appreciation of this world and what it has to offer. The spirit within us feeds and grows on our joy and appreciation of God's gifts for us that are found in our everyday lives. As we grow in faith we are able to identify His miracles and blessings and build a life that is based on knowing our Lord personally.

The Beginning of Miracles

GENESIS 1:1-4 READS, In the beginning God created the heaven and the earth. And the earth was without form, and void; and darkness was upon the face of the deep. And the Spirit of God moved upon the face of the waters. And God said, Let there be light: and there was light. And God saw the light, that it was good: and God divided the light from the darkness.

The first mention of the Holy Spirit is at the beginning when the Holy Spirit moved over the waters. The Holy Spirit was involved in the creation of the earth and all things that were created.

Genesis 2:7 reads, And the Lord God formed man of the dust of the ground, and breathed into his nostrils the breath of life; and the man became a living soul.

God created a man that was both a physical being and spiritual being with a soul. God's act of breathing life into Adam created a spiritual being capable of serving and having fellowship with God and the Holy Spirit. God's marvelous creation is a miracle that is beyond words and our comprehension.

We find ourselves on this beautiful planet, a precious jewel in space that is almost impossible to detect in a universe without limits. It is estimated there are 10 trillion planetary systems in the known universe. We live an estimated 80 years on this earth, but when we compared this life span to infinity or the age of this earth it is but a whisper in time. As with the rest of creation, we are like a flower that grows in the spring, flowers in the summer sun, and fades in the fall.

We are part of a miracle that requires us to use our imagination to begin to understand the opportunities that are available to us, so that we may live a life on a planet that provides us with countless miracles. This planet provides us with the air to breath, food to eat, shelter to protect from the elements, the joy of discovery, and the opportunity to praise God.

Life is a precious gift from God that we need to be continually thanking and praising God for on a daily basis. Our lives are beyond value and no amount of money can bring you back to life after you pass. We spend a short amount of time on this earth and we need to spend that time wisely. God has given us the gift of language to praise His name, the gift of song to sing of His blessing, the gift of sight, smell, taste, and hearing to appreciate all of his wonderful creations. He has given us a mind that is so complex we still do not completely understand how it works. We are able to reason, to solve complex problems, to create new and wonderful creations, to laugh and have fun, to love and to experience a whole realm of emotions.

We are blessed to be part of this miracle and we need to remember that we are to love our neighbor.

Matthew 22:37-40, reads, Jesus said unto him, "Thou shalt love the Lord thy God with all thy heart, and with all thy soul, and with all thy mind. This is the first and great commandment. And the second is like unto it, Thou shalt love thy neighbor as thyself. On these two commandments hang all the law and the prophets."

We are allowed to live this short period of time on this miraculous planet with the understanding that we will love our Lord with all of heart and mind and will love our neighbors as ourselves. What does that mean to the seven billion people living on this planet? It means each person is God's creation and has the opportunity to live for eternity with their Creator. The process is simple, to love God and to love your neighbor. This love will result in a life that has a profound effect on many of God's children. The birth, crucifixion, and resurrection of Jesus provided direct access to God and a personal relationship with Him and the Holy Spirit. Once we make the decision to believe in Jesus, we are released from the power of sin and the condemnation of the law.

Once we make that decision we become a new person capable of communing with the Holy Spirit. He changes our life in all ways by changing our priorities, our desires, and our emotions.

Galatians 5: 22-23 reads, But, the fruit of the Spirit is love, joy, peace, long suffering, gentleness, goodness, faith. Meekness, temperance: against such there is no law.

The Holy Spirit seeks to reproduce these values in the believer as they grow closer to their Lord and Savior. Goodness abhors evil and will cause a spiritual man to run from it when it is introduced in any situation. Those that are faithful will walk upright and will be faithful to their calling. Meekness is based on humility and will allow these Saints to deny self and allow others to be successful.

We struggle with the desires of the flesh on a daily basis and we need to recognize them for what they are and cast them aside. We live in the Spirit and we take each step in communion with Him.

God gave us all things that we would live a life that would honor His name and praise Him for all He has done. The breadth and depth of the blessing that we have received in this life are impossible to comprehend.

Why Some do not See God's Miracles

ADAM COULD NOT REMEMBER the positive results of obedience and the disastrous results of disobedience. We have short memories and are often focused on the daily tasks.

Matthew 6:25-29 reads, "Therefore I say unto you, Take no thought for your life, what ye shall eat, or what ye shall drink; nor yet for your body, what ye shall put on. Is not the life more than meat, and the body than raiment? Behold the fowls of the air, for they sow not, neither do they reap, nor gather into barns, yet your heavenly Father feedeth them. Are ye not much better than they? Which of you by taking thought can add one cubit unto his stature. And why take ye thought for raiment? Consider the lilies of the field, how they grow, they toil not, neither do they spin. And yet I say unto you, That even Solomon in all his glory was not arrayed like one of these."

Those that are consumed with worry about material possessions are destroying their relationship with their Lord. We are both physical and spiritual beings. For our Spirit to remain healthy and active it needs to spend time with its' Lord. A person that is continually focused on material goods will destroy their relationship with the Holy Spirit and lose direction and a sense of what is good and evil.

Matthew 6:33 reads, "But seek ye first the kingdom of God, and his righteousness, and all these things shall be added unto you.

Our first priority is to seek God's kingdom and all its righteousness. If we forget that simple principle we will slide into all kinds of evil and eventually lose the protection of our Father.

There is no room within many of the lives of people today for any type of spiritual belief. They are consumed by obtaining more and more materials goods and are continually worried about protecting their possessions. We live in a society where even at an early age children are exposed to this obsession of wearing expensive shoes and clothing. They are taught by their parents that an expensive possession will increase their status within their peer group. Unfortunately, business has taken advantage of this human weakness and targeted children with marketing gimmicks that promises status and attacks their self worth. This type of immoral pressure applied by business at children has resulted in children stealing, fighting, robbing, and even killing in some cases for shoes and clothing.

Satan and his demons are extremely cunning and will use greed, status, and material possessions as a weapon to destroy today's society. Today's society judges people by the amount of possessions they have accumulated.

John 12: 40 reads, He hath blinded their eyes, and hardened their heart; that they should not see with their eyes, nor understand with their heart, and be converted, and I should heal them.

The Jewish people refused to believe in Jesus even though He had performed many miracles. God warned Isaiah that most of the Jewish people would reject his ministry.

Isaiah 6:10 reads, Make the heart of this people fat, and make their ears heavy, and shut their eyes; lest they see with their eyes, and hear with their ears, and understand with their heart, and convert, and be healed.

There is no middle ground for those who wish not to commit to Christianity. You either love God or hate God. In this case, God hardened the hearts of the Jewish people because they refused to believe in Jesus and his many miracles.

Matthew 6:24 reads, "No man can serve two masters: for either he will hate the one, and love the other; or else he will hold to the one, and despise the other. Ye cannot serve God and mammon."

Once you make a decision to believe in Jesus and His miracles God is your master and He is in control of all your possessions. A person who makes a decision to believe in Jesus will be required to change his attitude about wealth and the accumulation of possessions here on earth. His focus changes from earthly possessions to building treasures in heaven. The treasures built in heaven will be there for eternity and are not subject to rust, disease, thief, or any other sin that Satan and demons use here on earth. A decision to refuse to believe in Jesus and His miracles results in the rejection of the Holy Ghost and His communion with a person's spirit. This opens the door for Satan and his demons to take up residency within a non-believer's life.

A Miracle Beyond Comprehension

SATAN AND HIS DEMONS would like you to believe that God is dead and that the earth is not a miracle. We live on an extremely rare jewel of a planet in a universe of hundreds of billions of planets. We live in a universe that is so vast that we cannot comprehend its size. It is by any definition a miracle beyond words. We have been so richly blessed to live and experience the wonders of this miracle called earth.

It is not by chance that God created this earth within a universe so immense that only God could find it and where it has been protected and nourished for billions of years. Astronomers estimate there are ten times more stars than grains of sand in all of earth's deserts and beaches. There are about 70 sextillion stars visible with modern telescopes. With the current rocket technology it would take an estimated 81,000 years to travel to Proxima Centauti the closest star.

It is not by chance that out of billions of dead planets in the universe this planet is able to support life.

It is not by chance that this planet orbits the sun at the appropriate distance and time to support life.

It is not by chance that this planet has the appropriate layers of atmosphere that support life.

It is not by chance that this planet has the appropriate magnetic field that protects it from solar flares.

It is not by chance that the oceans are filled with fish and other creatures that provide foods for billions of humans. It is estimated that over 120 billion people have lived on planet earth.

It is not by chance that the earth has different types of weather that provides fresh water and other nutrients for plants to grow and to provide food for billions of people and animals.

It is not by chance that this planet provides beautiful wonders to experience and explore.

It is not by chance that man was blessed with a mind and body capable of raising and harvesting food for billions of people.

It is not by chance that man and woman appeared on earth with the ability to love God, love each other, learn language, communicate, solve complex problems, have dominion over animals, and to be creative.

It is not by chance that we live on a planet where over 10,000 new animal species are discovered each year. It is estimated there are from 2 million to 50 million animal species on earth.

It is not by chance that we are spiritual beings and that our hearts are looking for our creator, the God of love, and the mercy where all of our needs will be met.

It is not by chance the earth's atmosphere is dense enough to protect us from 20 million meteors that enter it each day.

Obviously, these creations and miracles did not just appear by chance. No amount of time in a pool of primordial slime is going to evolve nothing into life. Even the basic forms of life are complex molecular cells that cannot be explained by natural selection.

Isaiah 42:5-6 reads, Thus saith God the Lord, he that created the heavens, and stretched them out; he that spread forth the earth, and that which cometh out of it; he that giveth breath unto the people upon it, and spirit to them that walk therein. I the Lord have called thee in righteousness, and will hold thine hand, and will keep thee; and give thee for a covenant of the people, for a light of the Gentiles.

Satan and his demons are working to discredit all of God's creation and miracles and to have man and woman focus on self. Man was made in God's image and was given free will. God wants man to freely decide if he wants to have a relationship with his Creator. It is only when man comes to the realization that his entire life was only possible with God's love and blessings that he understands that God has a plan for his life. It is man's decision to accept the gift of life by believing in the God and the gift of his only Son, Jesus.

Jesus lived his life as our example. Matthew 16:24 reads, then said Jesus unto his disciples, "If any man will come after me, let him deny himself, and take up his cross, and follow me." Christians throughout history and today have and will continue to experience persecution. This is primarily due to the fact Christianity requires a person to stand up against and denounce sin where ever it is practiced and present. Most of the disciples were persecuted for their beliefs and suffered the wrath of Satan and his demons as they poisoned and perverted the morals and values of society.

Jeremiah 17:9 reads, The heart is deceitful above all things and desperately wicked: who can know it? As was mentioned before, we need to remember that man's natural disposition is deceitful and cannot be trusted. Just as Lucifer fought God from the beginning he will continue to fight to discredit God and his many miracles.

Isaiah 14:12 reads, How art thou fallen from heaven, O Lucifer, son of the morning! How art thou cut down to the ground, which didst weaken the nations. For thou hast said in thine heart, I will ascend into heaven, I will exalt my throne above the stars of God: I will sit also upon the mount of the congregation, in the sides of the north: I will ascend above the heights of the clouds; I will be like the most high.

Lucifer was a powerful angel that was driven by a lust for power. He led a rebellion with other angels against God and was cursed and became the wicked one, the great thief and destroyer of mankind. Satan and his demons are still at work today trying to discredit and destroy God's many blessings and miracles through any means possible.

God's Reaction to Unbelief

THE BELIEVER IS UNDER God's grace through the death of His only Son Jesus the Christ. God is glorified through His creation of the earth, universe and many miracles. However, the unbeliever in his unbelief has refused to recognize God's many gifts to mankind.

Romans 1:18-24 reads, For the wrath of God is revealed from heaven against all ungodliness and unrighteousness of men, who hold that truth in unrighteousness. Because that which may be known of God is manifest in them; for God hath showed it unto them. For the invisible things of him from the creation of the world are clearly seen, being understood by the things that are made, even his eternal power and Godhead; so that they are without excuse. Because that, when they knew God, they glorified him not as God, neither were thankful; but became vain in their imaginations, and their foolish heart was darkened. Professing themselves to be wise, they became fools, And changed the glory of the uncorruptible God into an image made like to corruptible man, and to birds, and four-footed beasts, and creeping things. Wherefore God also gave them up to uncleanness through the lusts of their own hearts, to dishonor their own bodies between themselves.

The wrath of God is ever present and will come to be against all unrighteousness. Those that refuse to believe in God and to be thankful for his many blessings and glorify his name for all his creations will experience his wrath. The slow decay of social values and society is directly related to not believing in God and his wondrous works. As man becomes more puffed up in pride and begins to belittle God's creation he begins to fall future into moral decay.

He has broken all connection with God and his grace, the Holy Ghost no longer communes with his spirit, and he begins to drift in a sea of sin that knows no boundary. At this point man can no longer recognize sin and places his complete trust in self, money and what it can buy.

Unfortunately, today we see and hear few words of thankfulness for God's many blessings and his wondrous works in our daily news. We live in a country that was founded on Christian values, but has now been morally compromised to the point where it refuses to mention our Creator's name. It is truly a national embarrassment and extremely offensive to all Christians throughout the world. Unfortunately, it speaks volumes of how Satan has hardened the hearts of man.

There is a sequence of events that occurs when man no longer believes in his creator and refuses to give thanks and glorify his name. This progression begins with moral decay and ends with physical, spiritual, eternal death.

Psalm 105: 1-5 reads, O Give thanks unto the Lord; call upon his name: make know his deeds among the people. Sing unto him, sing psalms unto him, talk ye of all his wondrous works. Glory ye in his holy name: let the heart of them rejoice that seek the Lord. Seek the Lord, and his strength: seek his face evermore. Remember his marvelous works that he hath done; his wonders, and the judgments of his mouth.

We need to be actively giving thanks each day for His many blessings, through prayer, singing, praising, and rejoicing.

1 Chronicles 29:10-11 reads, Wherefore David blessed the Lord before all the congregation: and David said, Blessed be thou, Lord God of Israel our father, forever and ever. Thine, O lord, is the greatness, and the power, and the glory, and the victory, and the majesty: for all that is in the heaven and in the earth is thine; thine is the kingdom, O Lord, and thou art exalted as head above all.

We were created by God for the primary purpose of serving Him, praising his name, and thanking Him for the gift of His Son so that some day we may spend eternity with him.

2 Chronicles 5:13 reads, It came even to pass, as the trumpeters and singers were as one, to make one sound to be heard in praising and thanking the Lord; and when they lifted up their voice with trumpets and cymbals and instruments of music, and praised the Lord, saying, For he is good; for his mercy endureth for ever: that then the house was filled with a cloud, even the house of the Lord.

Psalm 113:3 reads, From the rising of the sun unto the going down of the same the Lord's name is to be praised.

King of Kings and Lord and Lords, God's grace is above the heavens, He cares for the poor and needy, His mercy endureth for ever, He gave his only son that we may live, He made the word flesh and dwelt among us, He is the Alpha and Omega, the beginning and the end. We are in awe of His greatness and pray in fear and complete reverence. We pray that our lives may reflect his grace, that the Holy Spirit may intercede for us, and that our prayers may be heard.

Prophecy for Miracles

THERE ARE MANY PROPHECIES in the Old Testament regarding Jesus' birth and his ministry. Isaiah was one of the most prominent prophets of the Old Testament and had a long life span from around 740 BC to 680BC. He lived in Judah and was instrumental in teaching that the Lord was responsible for their salvation and not their works and that they should live under God's covenant. They should be helping and encourage those with illnesses and inflictions. Isaiah prophesied that many would be healed of blindness, many would be healed that cannot speak and hear, and many would be healed that cannot walk.

Isaiah 35:4-6 reads, Say to them that are of a fearful heart, Be strong, fear not: behold, your God will come with vengeance, even God with a recompense, he will come and save you. Then the eyes of the blind shall be opened, and the ears of the deaf shall be unstopped. Then shall the lame man leap as a hart, and the tongue of the dumb sing: for in the wilderness shall water break out, and streams in the desert.

The Messiah did come and did live among his people for the purpose of providing salvation in a world that was and is God-defying and unrepentant. We live in a hostile world of over seven billion souls that is composed of two billion Christians and over one billion (1 in 6 people) have no religious affiliation. These souls have either rejected a belief in God, have not heard the gospel, or have been consumed by self and materialism.

Isaiah 53:3-5 reads, He is despised and rejected of men; a man of sorrows, and acquainted with grief: and we hid as it were our faces from him; he was despised, and we esteemed him not. Surely he hath borne our griefs, and carried our sorrows: yet we did esteem him stricken, smitten of God, and afflicted. But he was wounded for our transgressions; he was bruised for our iniquities: the chastisement of our peace was upon him; and with his stripes we are healed.

Isaiah prophesied that Jesus would come as a man and would be despised and carry the grief, sorrows of this world. He would heal them of their many afflictions and yet they would not esteem him. Jesus was a man of great sorrow because He gave His all for a people that rejected Him. Today, we live in a world that 1 in 6 has no religious affiliations and is completely lost.

Matthew 8:16-17 reads, When the even was come, they brought unto him many that were possessed with devils: and he cast out the spirits with his word, and healed all that were sick: That it might be fulfilled which was spoken by Isaiah the prophet, saying, HIMSELF TOOK OUR INFIRMITIES, AND BARE OUR SICKNESSES.

The world and man has received the greatest gift of all and that is to spend eternity with their Creator. It is free, yet many do not accept this gift due to Satan and his influence. We are in a daily struggle with demons that have great influences over businesses that sells debauchery and man's ultimate destruction for a profit.

Jeremiah another Old Testament prophet also prophesied many of the events that occurred during the time Jesus was here on earth. His ministry lasted from about 640BC to 586BC and his message was focused on the final judgment and the new covenant.

Jeremiah 31:31-32 reads, Behold, the days come, saith the Lord, that I will make a new covenant with the house of Israel, and with the house of Judah: Not according to the covenant that I made with their fathers in the day that I took them by the hand to bring them out of the land of Egypt; which my covenant they brake, although I was a husband unto them, saith the Lord:

Jeremiah is prophesying that a new covenant will be made between God and man and that it will include the Gentiles. This covenant will include the entire world and will include all of mankind. This covenant will be based on the sacrifice of the Son of God for the forgiveness of all of man's sin. God's grace knows no limits and is beyond our comprehension.

Matthew 26:28-29 reads, "For this is my blood of the new testament, which is shed for many for the remission of sins. But I say unto you, I will not drink henceforth of the fruit of the vine, until that day when I drink it new with you in my Father's kingdom."

The passing of the cup was used by the Jewish family during the Passover meal. It signifies and reminds us of the God's blessings and protection through obedience as He led the Hebrews from Egypt. This also represents redemption, praise, acceptance, and salvation. Jesus calls the cup "the new covenant in My blood".

After the Ascension of Jesus

FOR THE NEXT FEW centuries Israel and the Jewish people remain under the severe rule of the Roman government. The Apostles were in danger of being imprisoned and left Jerusalem and were scattered throughout the area surrounding the Mediterranean. About 70 AD the Jewish people revolted against the Roman rule that resulted in severe punishment. The Roman General Titus laid siege to Jerusalem and destroyed the Temple and killed many Jews. The Jews revolted again against Rome about 123 AD and again Jerusalem was destroyed and its people were slaughtered. Emperor Hadrian of Rome destroyed much of the city and killed thousands. Many of the Jewish people left Israel for fear of losing their lives and relocated to many different counties.

It was not until about 400 AD that Israel and Jerusalem falls under Persian rule and then under the Byzentine Empire. At about 636 AD Israel and Jerusalem fell under Muslim rule and the Dome on Rock was built over where the Jewish Temple was located.

Israel and Jerusalem fell under many different rules after that point in time. The Crusaders from 1099 to 1244, Ottoman Turks about 1517, Egypt 1822, Britain 1917 after WWI. It isn't until 1947 that the United Nations adopts a partition plan for the establishment of a Jewish State.

The Quran was assembled as a book during the reign of Caliph Uthman about 644 AD. The book is considered the immutable word of God by Muslims and the actual application of various laws and its punishments varies from country to country. The strict and most severe applications of Islam seem to be found in Iran, Afghanistan, and Somalia. The view of Christians and Jews varies depending on the age of the verse within the Quran. The early verses viewed Christians and Jews in a more positive light. There also seems to be some similarities between Christianity and Islam. Obviously, the Jewish Torah, Septuagint, and many New Testament books were available during the time period that the Quran was assembled.

The biggest problem in reading any historical document is taking information out of context. The Quran was written during a time when the Muslim society was composed of tribes and addresses many of the issues related to individual tribal conflicts. There appears to be many conflicts and some persecution of Muslims during this time and the Quran addresses how the tribe should react to this persecution. It should also be noted, that forgiveness and repentance is also addressed and when it should be applied.

Summary

IT APPEARS IN THE three years of Jesus' ministry only a few of Jesus' miracles were actually recorded in the Bible. There may be a number of reasons why this occurred. Jesus would often ask that no one would tell of these wondrous works so as to prevent unwanted attention by the Jewish and government leadership. As the years past, Jesus' reputation grew along with the size of the crowds and the number of witnesses. In the third year some of the crowds were so great that Jesus and disciples had to withdraw to get rest. As the crowds grew greater in size so did the number of witnesses to these miracles and the amount and accuracy of the documentation. In many cases there were hundreds of witnesses to these miracles.

The first of these miracles was the miracle of changing water into wine at the wedding that was attended by some of the disciples and Mary the mother of Jesus. Mary notified Jesus of the situation knowing He could provide a solution. Jesus takes this issue to notify His mother that his ministry has not yet begun and to allow His disciples to witness His power and grace and to allow them to grow in faith. Jesus' transition to full time ministry did change His relationship to both Mary and His disciples and make them finally realize He was the Messiah.

Shortly after beginning his ministry Jesus and the disciples travel through Samaria where they meet a Samaritan woman at Jacob's well. This encounter begins to bring into focus and defines Jesus' ministry and how He views all people and their daily lives. Jesus' vision is completely contrary to how the Jews value and treat all Samarians, since the Jews hated and avoided Samaria and its people. Jesus' willingness to speak to this woman who has had five husbands creates a situation that is not going to be understood by the Jewish community. After speaking with Jesus for some time this woman believes Jesus to be the Messiah and because of her testimony many more Samarians believed in Jesus that he is the Savior of the world. Jesus has established an example for all to follow and that we need to accept all people as they are regardless of their history and ask them simply to believe. The disciples begin to understand that Jesus came to save the sinner and is asking them to present the gospel to all men throughout the entire world. Jesus welcomes all people where they are in their daily lives.

In the second year of Jesus' ministry great mercy and compassion is shown to the people with many healings of different infirmities throughout the area of Galilee. God's eternal mercy is reaching out to us all within all of our needs each day. However, these miracles were not going unnoticed by the Jewish leaders. While healing one paralyzed man Jesus said "Thy sins are forgiven thee". The scribe after hearing this considered this to be blasphemy and began plotting against Him.

Jesus as the Messiah was both showing mercy by healing many and at the same time revealing His plan for salvation for people that are living from day to day with no hope. The Jews were following the law and their rules to the letter and trying to apply their laws and rules to a man that was actually their Lord.

The disciples were beginning to realize that nothing was impossible with the man they were traveling with. They have seen Him heal those that were sick, paralyzed, and raised people from the dead and now they see that winds and seas are under his command. The disciples and Jesus were on the Sea of Galilee in a small boat when a severe storm suddenly appeared and threaten to capsize the boat. The disciples woke Jesus from a deep sleep and asked for his help. Jesus seeing the panic in the faces of his disciples simply said, "Peace, be still". Immediately the wind stopped and the sea became calm.

Psalms 29:3-4 reads, The voice of the Lord is upon the waters: the God of glory thundereth: the Lord is upon many waters. The voice of the Lord is powerful; the voice of the Lord is full of majesty.

Job 12: 7-9 reads, But ask now the beasts, and they shall teach thee, and the fowls of the air, and they shall tell thee: Or speak to the earth, and it shall teach thee; and the fishes of the sea shall declare unto thee. Who knoweth not in all these that the hand of the Lord hath wrought this?

The disciples are learning that the forces of nature are at God's disposal to use as He wills. He is able to cause fish to collect in their nets until they break, stop the wind from blowing, and calm a stormy sea with only saying a few words.

The disciples also learned about faith and how important it is for a miracle to take place. Faith was the primary reason why healing took place for the Centurion soldier's servant and the women that touch the coat of Jesus. Both of these people were confident without a doubt that Jesus had the power to heal. In their minds it was simply a matter of getting Him to stop and hear their request. Jesus said after listening to the Centurion soldier, "Verily I say unto you, I have not found so great a faith, no not in Israel." Jesus was making the point that this Gentile soldier's faith in Him was greater than the faith displayed by all Jews within Israel. He was also establishing the fact that His ministry will be received by many of great faith throughout the world. Man is both a physical and spiritual being. However, many do not recognize the spiritual part of their being and go throughout their entire lives without allowing their spirit to rejoice in God's love. They live within the limits of the physical and believe only what they see, feel, hear, and smell. God's directions are generally from the Holy Spirit and are not heard with the ear, seen with the eye, or felt by a touch. Consequently, faith is the primary component for the spiritual part of a person to live and rejoice in God's direction and grace. Growing and nurturing the Spirit is a daily process that requires prayer, study, and obedience. Those that do not care for their spirit and its condition fall prey to the influences of Satan and his demons.

A second miracle of faith occurs with a woman that had been under many physicians' care for many years with no cure. She also believed that if she simply touched Jesus' coat she would be healed. In this situation the women was healed simply because she believed she would be healed. Jesus through his omniscience knew this women's condition, her faith, and allowed this healing to occur. Jesus did not need to address this woman as He did with others, because she was already at that place in her faith where she knew the healing would be completed as soon as she touched His coat.

Hebrews 11:6 reads, But without faith it is impossible to please Him, for he that cometh to God must believe that He is, and that He is a rewarder of them that diligently seek Him.

Hebrews 11:7 reads, By faith Noah, being warned of God of things not seen as yet, moved with fear, prepared an ark to the saving of his house; by the which he condemned the world, and became heir of the righteousness which is by faith.

Noah was a man of great faith. He was obedient to God's command and built an ark without ever seeing rain. His labor and obedience resulted in saving his family and achieving righteousness in God's eyes.

It appears a major portion of the recorded miracles in the Bible occurred in the third year of Jesus' ministry. The miracles varied from healing the blind to casting out demons to the resurrection of Jesus. This year was also a time of miraculous miracles where all of mankind should be on their knees giving unending praise and thanks to our Lord Jesus Christ for His unspeakable, astounding, and incredible gift to all of mankind.

Jesus was constantly traveling showing God's mercy, healing and teaching the message of salvation. Great crowds of people begin to follow Him asking for the healing of many different infirmities. On two occasions He feeds great crowds of 4,000 and 5,000 people with only small portions of food donated from the crowds. However, many of these followers were only interested in the blessings and are not interested in the message of salvation and did not believe Jesus was their Savior.

Another major miracle that occurred in the third year of Jesus' ministry was the transfiguration. Jesus leads Peter, James, and John to a mountain top where the transfiguration is completed.

Mark 9:2-4 reads, And after six days Jesus taketh with him Peter, and James, and John, and leadeth them up unto a high mountain apart by themselves: and he was transfigured before them. And his raiment became shining, exceeding white as snow; so as no fuller on earth can white them. And there appeared unto them Elijah with Moses: and they were talking with Jesus.

Jesus had chosen his witnesses (Peter, James, and John) to be present at His transfiguration. It is understood that God's transfiguration of Jesus was for the preparation of a sinless sacrifice and the resurrection of a Savior. Also present at the transfiguration was Elijah and Moses. Elijah a great prophet was representing and bearing witness to the prophecy that a Messiah would come to offer salvation to the entire world. Moses the man who led the Israelites out of Egypt and delivered the law and the 10 commandments was also present representing God's law and direction. The Bible is composed of both the New and Old Testament. They complement each other in explaining and presenting the love of God for the entire world.

The Apostle James, a witness to the transfiguration later wrote in James 2: 10-11. For whosoever shall keep the whole law, and yet offend in one point, he is guilty of all. For he that said, Do not commit adultery, said also, Do not kill. Now if thou commit no adultery, yet if thou kill, thou are become a transgressor of the law.

The Apostle James a witness with Apostle Peter and John of the transfiguration of Jesus confirmed that the law is still in place and has not been replaced by any other.

The Apostle John also a witness to the transfiguration wrote later in 1 John 2: 4-6. He that saith, I know him, and keepeth not his commandments, is a liar, and truth is not in him. But whoso keepeth his word, in him verily is the love of God perfected: hereby know we that we are in him. He that saith he abideth in him ought himself also so to walk, even as he walked.

The Apostle John is also confirming the law is still in place and needs to be followed if a person loves God.

The Apostle Peter a man of great love for Jesus also wrote in 2 Peter 3:2. That ye may be mindful of the words which were spoken before by the holy prophets, and of the commandment of us the apostles of Lord and Savior.

The Apostle Peter was confirming the inspiration of the Old Testament and the words spoken by the Apostles as within God's authority.

All three Apostles were witnesses to the miracle of transfiguration of Jesus and later confirmed that the Old Testament and the law are to be recognized as Gods' inspired word.

As is written in Hebrews: 8:10, For this is the covenant that I will make with the house of Israel. After those days, saith the lord; I will put my laws into their mind, and write them in their hearts; and I will be to them a God, and they shall be to me a people.

We need to remember if we love God we will keep His commandments. Society, governments, and some churches no longer recognize the Old Testament as God's inspired word and refuse to recognize the Ten Commandments. We need to be extremely careful of false teachers that are out to deceive us for their own purposes. We are strangers to this world and traveling to our final resting place in heaven.

Jesus was asked what was the greatest of the commandment and He replied as follows:

Matthew 22: 36-40 reads, Master, which is the great commandment in the law? Jesus said unto him, "Thou shalt love the Lord thy God with all thy heart, and with all thy soul, and with all thy mind. This is the first and great commandment. And the second is like unto it, Thou shalt love thy neighbor as thyself. On these two commandments hang all the law and the prophets." From these two laws flows an endless stream of blessings. As servants of God we are commissioned to go into the world and love our neighbor. We are commissioned to help those that cannot help themselves, the poor, the widow, the hungry, and those in need of shelter.

Many miracles occur during the third year of Jesus ministry. We read of the blind, deaf, demon possessed, leapers, and other infirmities all being healed by Jesus as He and disciples traveled throughout the land. We also read of the raising of Lazarus a man who had been dead for four days. There is no possible explanation for this man coming back to life after four days other than a miracle created by God. With this miracle and others Jesus was revealing his power of over death and was reflecting Gods' grace and mercy.

The death of Jesus on the cross and His resurrection was one of the last miracles completed during his lifetime.

Only God could provide the sinless sacrifice of His only son for the forgiveness of sins for the entire world. The only request from God was that man would believe in His son and the perfect sacrifice that was made. Jesus was the perfect sacrifice and is the new covenant that was completed for all mankind. Jesus lived a sinless life in complete obedience to God's word and was therefore the sinless lamb that was crucified for each person.

The resurrection was the act that defeated Satan and his power over death for all of mankind.

Ephesians 2:6-9 reads, And hath raised us up together, and made us sit together in heavenly places in Christ Jesus. That in the ages to come he might show the exceeding riches of his grace in his kindness toward us through Christ Jesus. For by grace are ye saved through faith; and that not of yourselves; it is the gift of God. Not of works, least any man should boast.

Satan was defeated with the resurrection of Jesus and at the same time we were given authority over the power Satan and his demons. We were given free will and the power to make our own decisions over our daily lives. We can either live an obedient life following God's word or a sin filled life, the choice is ours.

Luke 10:19, reads, Jesus said, "Behold, I give unto you power to tread on serpents and scorpions, and over all the power of the enemy: and nothing shall by any means hurt you."

Satan today is like a roaring lion and we need to be always alert of his influences throughout our lives. Satan is able to keep people separate from God by taking advantage of their weaknesses. Many people today are self-absorbed, greedy, and looking to acquire more material goods. Satan will use this temptation of wealth to lead people into destruction. Satan will also use knowledge as with the theory of evolution to cause people not to believe in God and reject any idea to live a moral life.

After Jesus' resurrection he appeared to a number of the Apostles over a 40 day period for the purpose of strengthening their faith and allowing them to grow in understanding that His resurrection was completed.

Mark 16: 12-14 reads, After that he appeared in another form unto two of them, as they walked, and went into the country. And they went and told it unto the residue: neither believed they them. Afterward he appeared unto the eleven as they sat at meat, and upbraided them with their unbelief and hardness of heart, because they believed not them which had seen him after he was risen.

The Apostles were traumatized and in fear after the crucifixion of Jesus their teacher and Savior. They met behind locked doors for fear the Jewish leaders may accuse them of some crime and take their lives. The 40 day time period between the resurrection and the ascension was also a time where many miracles were wittiness by hundreds if not thousands of people. The Gospels of John and Matthew provides more detail about the miracle of catching fish and Jesus appearances to Peter, Thomas and others.

Conclusion

THERE ARE AN ESTIMATED 318 million people living in the United States of which 83% claim to be Christian. But yet, much of the social media that is produced in the US and distributed throughout the world is offensive to most religions. Satan and his demons have distorted our laws and regulations to the point where any type of perverted and deviant organization and its practices are protected by U.S. law. In addition, many movies and television programs are offensive to many US citizens.

We live during a time when being politically correct and conforming to social standards is the generally acceptable moral view. Many of our churches no longer teach the Old Testament and are no longer willingly to explain or define sin. In fact, some churches teach that we should only be involved in what makes us feel good and makes us happy. The study of Jesus and his ministry makes us realize we are to show his love by sharing the gospel to all people. If they reject the message we are to move on to the next person. We are not to judge least we be judged.

Jesus' ministry, teachings, and miracles were for all mankind. He did not avoid or exclude any person. In fact, he addressed and engaged with all people regardless of their position or standing within the society. He was hated and despised by the Jewish community because of his continual association with those that were considered undesirable or did not follow Jewish law and rules. In fact, Jesus made a point not to follow all the laws and rules of the Jewish people when they were in conflict with the commandment to love your neighbor. Even though Jesus delivered great blessings, miraculous miracles, and mercy to hundreds of Jewish people the Jewish leadership refused to believe that He was their Messiah.

Only God is able to provide a way to save people from their sins and allow them to spend eternity in heaven. God offered his only Son, the only man that ever lived a sinless life, as a sinless sacrifice for all mankind. The only condition was that they believe that Jesus was their Messiah. And, if you love Jesus you will keep his commandments.

Yes, Jesus came to save all of mankind from all their sins. He ministered to all of mankind and did not exclude anyone and consequently, millions of souls have been saved. He is continually meeting people today where they are in their lives and instructing them as to how to live a Christ like life that would open a door to an eternity of blessings.

Christianity is the belief that God gave his only Son as a sinless sacrifice for all of mankind. This act of love, mercy, and forgiveness is for every person and is available throughout a person's life regardless of what this person said or did. However, there are many that refuse this gift of eternal life because of other religious beliefs. In fact, there are about 140 countries throughout the world where Christians experience some type of discrimination for their belief. Christian churches are being burned and Christians are being killed and imprisoned in countries like, North Korea, Somalia, Pakistan, Nigeria, Egypt, Burma, and many more. Many of the countries where this hatred for Christians is present, is where the Islamic faith is practiced. The Quran states, "All Christians will be burned in the fire".

Some that follow Islam see the US and the West as the serpent's head of all evil. As the West falls deeper into moral decay the Radical Islamist see themselves as killers of evil and are free with a clear conscience to kill Westerners and Christians. The Jews and the Christians rejected Mohammed as the promised Messiah and quickly experienced his wrath and hated.

This basic element of respect for self and another person is missing throughout the entire world. This problem is the greatest in the West where the family unit has been destroyed after years of neglect. Respect is best taught within the family unit where children are parented on a daily basis. Unfortunately, the family unit in some cases has been missing for generations and the basic understanding of morals and respect has also been lost. In many cases, generation after generation of children are being raised by adults that have no respect or interest in sending these children to the church for religious training.

Our prayers as Christians should be for these families that are struggling to survive in a world that has no respect for the family and their moral wellbeing. We pray for the young that feel they have no hope and no future. Satan is like a roaming lion looking to devour our youth as they roam the streets searching for someone that will love them just as they are.

However, God is actively engaged in executing righteousness and judgment for the oppressed. God is also slow to anger and shows great mercy towards his people. His mercy is beyond measure and is never ending.

Psalms 103: 6-13 reads, The Lord executeth righteousness and judgment for all that are oppressed. He made known his ways unto Moses, his acts unto the children of Israel. The lord is merciful and gracious, slow to anger, and plenteous in mercy. He will not always chide: neither will he keep his anger for ever. He hath not dealt with us after our sins; nor rewarded us according to our iniquities. For as the heaven is high above the earth, so great is his mercy toward them that fear him. As far as the east is from the west, so far hath he removed our transgressions from us. Like as a father pitieth his children, so the Lord pitieth them that fear him.

God revealed his glory to Moses.

Exodus 34: 6-7 reads, And the Lord passed by before him, and proclaimed, the Lord God, merciful and gracious, long-suffering, and abundant in goodness and truth. Keeping mercy for thousands, forgiving iniquity and transgression and sin, and that will by no means clear the guilty; visiting the iniquity of the fathers upon the children, and upon the children's children, unto the third and the fourth generation.

We cannot forget that man was created in God's image and that we need to love one another and treat each other with respect. We ask God to renew our minds and develop in us His tender compassionate spirit for all those in need. We should be following God's Spirit as He prepares us and those that come our way that are in need of His Grace and miracles. We step out in faith knowing that God will provide in us the ability to provide direction and support.

Remember God gave His only Son that all men may be forgiven of all sin and have everlasting life. All men are God's creation and all are an integral part of God's plan for His kingdom.

We are given such a divine, God-given glimpses into the future that reveals to us more of His plan. What intense truth, what divine meaning there is in God's creative words: "Let us make man in our image, after our likeness!" To show forth the likeness of the Invisible, to be partaker of the divine nature, to share with God his rule of the universe, is man's destiny. His place is indeed one of unspeakable glory. Standing between two eternities, the eternal purpose in which we were predestinated to be conformed to the image of the first-born son, and the eternal realization of that purpose, when we shall be like him in his glory. We hear the voice from every side: O ye image-bearers of God! on the way to share the glory of God and of Christ, live a God-like, live a Christ-like life! Written by—Andrew Murray

Luke 22: 39-43 reads, And he came out, and went, as he was wont, to the Mount of Olives: and his disciples also follow him. And when he was at the place, he said unto them, "Pray that ye enter not into temptation." And he was withdrawn from them about a stone's cast, and kneeled down, and prayed, Saying, "Father, if thou be willing, remove this cup from me: nevertheless not my will, but thine, be done." And there appeared an angel unto him from heaven, strengthening him.

We pray in Christ's name, recognizing that we are subject to His will in our lives. He has a plan for our lives and we need to be continually in prayer. If His words are within your being you will experience his direction.

John 15:7 reads, "If ye abide in me, and my words, ye shall ask what ye will, and it shall be done unto you."

To abide in God's word means being obedient to His commandments; loving God with all your heart and mind, loving your neighbor, and to bring forth fruit.

Notes

References throughout out the book are from the King James translation of the Holy Bible.

Spurgeon, Charles H. *Spurgeon's Sermon Notes: Over 250 Sermons Including Notes, Commentary and Illustrations*. David Otis Fuller, ed. Grand Rapids, MI: Kregel, 1990.

Buswell, James Oliver Jr. Problems in the Prayer Life: From a Pastor's Question Box. Chicago: The Bible Institute, 1928.

Geikie, Cunningham. *The Life and Words of Christ*. New York: Appleton and Company, 1879.

Brenton, Lancelot C. *The Septuagint with Apocypha: Greek and English*. Hendrickson, 1986.